Don't Go Barefoot
to a Snake Stompin'

Don't Go Barefoot to a Snake Stompin'

and Other "RONdom Thoughts"

by Ron Birk

Hope you get a kick out of this!

Ron Birk

LANGMARC
PUBLISHING
AUSTIN, TEXAS

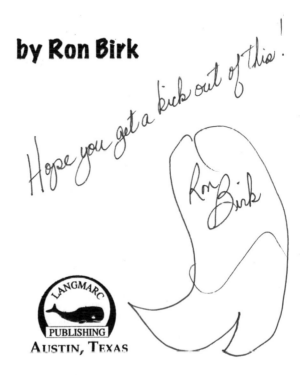

DON'T GO BAREFOOT
TO A SNAKE STOMPIN':
AND OTHER "RONDOM THOUGHTS"
BY RON BIRK

Cover Artist: David Espurvoa

Copyright © 2004 Ron Birk
Cover Graphics: Michael Qualben
Cover Photo: Don Anders

First Edition Printing: 2004
Printed in the United States of America

PUBLISHED BY
LangMarc Publishing
P.O. 90488, Austin, Texas 78709
1-800-864-1648

Cataloging in Publication: 2004092364
ISBN: 1-880292-270 $11.95

DEDICATION

Writing columns is a one person endeavor. Putting a collection of columns into book form is a team effort. My thanks to the all-star lineup of Alberta, David, Lois, and Michael who each made valuable contributions to this project. YEA TEAM!

TABLE OF CONTENTS

INTRODUCTION

What you are reading was once a blank page. No words. No thoughts. Just a white ("blanc" in French), colorless, unmarked piece of paper. An empty, barren, vacant void.

All writing begins with a blank page. The writer's task is to fill in that blank.

In 1980 I began writing "RONDOM THOUGHTS" as a "blank-filling" feature in *The Southern Lutheran*, the monthly publication of the former Southern District of The American Lutheran Church. It continues today in *The Vista*, the official newspaper of the Southwestern Synod of the Evangelical Lutheran Church in America. For eight years during that period, a weekly version of the column appeared in various community papers in Texas.

As an introduction to this third collection of "RONDOM THOUGHTS," I share some reflections on the frustrations and elations of creative writing.

"Writing is easy," observes Gene Fowler. "All you do is stare at a blank sheet of paper until drops of blood form on your forehead."

Far too often over the years I have sat, pen poised over blank paper, with a fast approaching deadline breathing down my neck, and all I can do is—draw a blank!

The only words this blank mind confronting blank paper can seem to produce are, "Those blankety-blank blanks!"

These are the times I am reminded of the words of another writer: "A blank page is God's way of showing you how hard it is to be God."

Kathleen Morris, my favorite current spiritual author, comments in her book *The Cloister Walk*, (Riverhead Books, NY, 1996) "No matter how much I've written or published, I always return to the blank page...An important aspect of monastic life has been described as 'attentive waiting.' I think it's also a fair description of the writing process. Once, when I was asked, 'What is the main thing a poet does?' I was inspired to answer, 'We wait.'"

Poets, columnists, creative writers of any kind —all are greatly dependent upon "attentive waiting." Blank minds don't fill blank pages. To create, writers need to be tuned in to the creator and to the creator's creation and creatures. All the receivers of the body, the mind, and the soul turned on. One's entire being on tiptoes, vigilantly alert for incoming insight and inspiration.

This, however, is not easy. It can be the pits. Even for Biblical poets like David, whose frustration is expressed eloquently in Eugene Peterson's translation of Psalm 40:1, "I waited and waited and waited for God."

But David's patience does pay off. "At last he (God) looked; finally he listened." "He drew me up from the desolate pit... (And) put a new song in my mouth." (Psalm 40:2-3, NRSV)

As a writer, I have learned, like David, to be a waiter. I wait for the Lord to fill in the blanks in my mind, so I can fill in the blanks on this page, which in turn just may fill in some of the blanks in the reader's life.

Writers are waiters. Waiters for the creator. Waiters (servers) upon the readers.

Writing is by nature a solitary craft. But, as Kathleen Norris points out, it is paradoxically communal. The purpose of writing is not completed until it is read.

To repeat what I wrote in the introduction to a previous collection of these columns, "Without readers, writers labor in vain. Without you, we writers would be like actors without an audience, teachers without students, cooks without eaters. It is you sitting in your chair reading that keeps me at my desk writing.

"Turning a blank sheet of paper into a page full of words is often a lonely, frustrating task. But when someone reads those words and is inspired, enlightened, or entertained by them, all my toil is worthwhile. What you are doing right now as a reader affirms what I have been doing as a writer. And I appreciate it.

"So you read on. And I'll write on."

- Ron Birk

WE ARE HERE TODAY BECAUSE THEY WERE HERE YESTERDAY

On a hot October Sunday afternoon in the last year of the 20th century, a mini-motorcade of cars and pickup trucks bounced down a rocky ranch road 14 miles west of Llano, Texas. The destination? A small family cemetery island in a sea of scraggly mesquites.

A mournful funeral procession? No. This was a joyful pilgrimage to celebrate a family tree planted on American soil 150 years before. Branches of that tree, which had spread far from its original site beside the Llano River, were gathering to remember and honor their roots with the unveiling of a new marker. Its simple inscription read: "BIRK CEMETERY – *Unserliebe Verwandtschaft* (Our Loving Relations)."

In 1849 Johannes and Elizabeth Birk completed their arduous journey from Germany and began to make a new home on the foreboding frontier of Central Texas. Among their children was nine-year-old Jacob, who later in 1876 purchased the ranch where the present cemetery is located. There he settled in 1882 with his wife, Sophie. And there, in graves grubbed out of granite gravel ground, they remain today.

Jacob's parents are buried on their original place across the river. However, since that land is no longer in the Birk family, Johannes (John) and Elizabeth's headstones were relocated beside their son in 1979.

4

Standing by the grave markers of my great and great-great grandparents was a moving experience for this fifth generation Texas Birk. It was a time for the words "family" and "ancestors," "heritage" and "roots" to come alive with vivid meaning and depth.

Charles Dobbins caught my feelings when he wrote: "If you want to know the greatest miracle of all, you are looking at it. I WAS BORN!

"I came from 2 people. Who came from 4 people. Who came from 8 people. Who came from 16 people. Who came from 32 people. Who came from 64 people. Who came from 128 people. Who came from 256 people. Who came from 512 people. Who came from 1024 people.

"If you go back to 1492 when Columbus discovered America, I have approximately 60,000 people who produced me. If I go back one more generation, it's 120,000. Then 240,000. Then 480,000. Then 960,000.

"It's hard to realize, but from the comparatively short time in history of the mid-1300's, it took over a million people to produce me!

"You may not believe that we are brothers and sisters in the Family of Christ, but I can guarantee you are my cousin!"

I don't know about you, but I need to be reminded regularly of that basic truth of life. You and I did not just pop into history without any roots. We are only here because of a lot of other people were here long before us. People who passed on their name, their genes, their life to us.

Ashleigh Brilliant speaks for me when he says, "I would like to thank all the people who kept the world going until I got here."

But another basic fact of life is—most of those people who kept the world going until we got here are gone.

Now it is our turn on the stage of life. Our chance to make our contribution to history. Just as we have ancestors, someday we will be ancestors. Just as we have a heritage, someday we will leave a heritage. Someday people who come after us will look back and thank us for keeping the world going until they got here.

The Psalmist has written, "God setteth the solitary in families." (68:6 JKV) None of us live a life alone free from the influence of our families, present or past. I am a child of my parents, my grandparents, and all the "greats" and "great-greats" before them.

In the same way, I am a parent. Not only of my children, but also my grandchildren, and all the little "greats" and "great-greats" that will follow.

That is what being part of family is all about—continuity with the ages, being a link in the chain of history. And that is why such an event as this is so important. It reminds me of my connection to a family and the contribution those family ties have in making me me.

So thank you Johannes and Elizabeth. Thank you Jacob and Sophie. Thank you for the part you played in making me who I am—Ron BIRK!

THANKS FOR THE TURKEYS

"One of the hardest things for me to believe about the Bible is that there were only two turkeys on the Ark!" fumed old pastoral friend Tex Luther. "There had to be more than that to produce all the turkeys I've dealt with lately in my church."

"Having some problems, are you?" I asked.

"Boy howdy, am I," he said. "No longer is Cuero the 'Turkey Capital of Texas.' Our church now has that distinction. I feel like I've quit shepherding sheep and gone to tending turkeys."

"And by 'turkeys,' you mean..."

"People who are aggravating, irritating, pesky pests. People who get my dander up, bend me plumb out of shape, ruffle my feathers, put a burr under my saddle, make me want to throw a hissy fit, and any other ol' Texas saying you can think of for angry, mad or upset."

After blowing off his steam, there was a long pause as Tex simmered down. When he seemed calm, cool, and collected again, Tex gave me a wry grin and said, "Got any advice for this frustrated turkey-tender?"

"As a matter of fact, I do. Your situation reminds me of a couple of quotes I saw in a recent issue of *The Joyful Noiseletter*. One had to do with changing a 'grrrr-attitude'—which you seem to have—into 'gratitude.' The other suggests a way to do that, 'May this Thanksgiving help you to give thanks for all the turkeys in your life.'"

"Hey," said Tex, "If I had my druthers, I'd prefer to give thanks for *no* turkeys in my life."

Laughing, I replied, "Me, too. But I'm not sure we have that choice. It's like the old story about a new boss who wanted to make sure his employees would like him. So for Thanksgiving he gave them each a turkey. Then he assured them, 'As long as I'm around you will always have a turkey.'"

"So what you're telling me," said Tex, "is instead of being in the rat race, I'm in a turkey trot?"

"Right. The turkeys ye shall have with you always. This means we pastors can't shirk the irking jerks that lurk in kirk work."

"O, how poetic, Pastor *Birk*," Tex said with a smirk. "But, even though I hate to admit it, you're probably right. However, in my present state of mind, the only thing I can find to be grateful about the turkeys around me is to thank God I'm not like them!"

"Well, that's a start," I said. "We all need negative examples. People who are models of how *not* to act. Some of the greatest lessons I've learned in life have come from watching the mistakes other people have made and the consequences of those blunders. Then vowing never to slip up like that myself.

"Another thing about being thankful for the turkeys is the challenge they present us."

"How's that?" asked Tex.

"It's easy to live with nice people." I went on. "But if it weren't for the turkeys, we might never have the opportunity to practice those great Christian virtues of patience, self-control, tolerance, forgiveness, mercy, etc. And most of all, turkeys challenge us to love, really love, with all the suffering and sacrifice that go along with the deepest Christian meaning of that word."

Tex thought about this for a minute. Then he mused, "Be thankful for turkeys, huh? Well, I asked for advice. But let's stop there. I don't think I could handle it if you told me that what Jesus really said was, 'Feed my turkeys!'"

APPLES AND RAINBOWS

A young reporter was sent out to interview a man celebrating his 100th birthday. When he arrived, he found the elderly gentleman sitting on his front porch in his rocking chair smoking a cigar. After introductions and small talk, the reporter began his interview.

"I see you're smoking a cigar. Is that to celebrate this special day?"

"Nope. Do it every day."

"How many a day?"

"Don't count. But I'd guess about a dozen."

"Do you drink, too?"

"A little. Probably only a pint or so a day."

"Women?"

"Well, sonny, had me three wives. Fourteen children. Twenty-eight grandchildren. Reckon by now it's 'bout forty-three great-grandchildren."

"That's remarkable," commented the reporter in awe. "With that kind of lifestyle, how have you managed to survive 100 years?"

Without a pause the centenarian replied, "Maybe 'cause I never wasted no energy resisting temptation."

Spoken like a true son of Eve. In the Garden of Eden our first mother didn't waste much time resisting the temptation of the forbidden fruit. And she promptly passed on her appetite for apples to all her descendants.

I don't know about you, but sometimes I get the feeling that life is just one big apple orchard. Temptations are all around me.

Now I'm no dummy. I can read the "No Trespassing" signs. I am fully aware the "Violators Will Be Prosecuted" is no idle threat, personally knowing trespassers who have been caught and suffered the consequences.

But, like Eve, I see "how beautiful the tree was, and how good its fruit would be to eat" (Genesis 3:6 GNB), and I succumb. With a hefty pull and a hearty bite, the apple is off the tree and between my teeth.

H. L. Mencken was right, "Temptation is an irresistible force at work on a moveable body."

After giving in to my innate weakness, my kinship to Eve continues. The appetite has been appeased, but the conscience is uneased. After the gluttony comes the guilt. After the repast comes the remorse.

What next? Thomas Merton identified the dilemma when he wrote, "Once the apple is plucked, you can't put it back on the tree."

My experience has been to forget Eve and remember Noah.

Throw the apple core on the ground, look up through the dark shade of the orchard, and feast your eyes on the rainbow. That bright arc over a cloudy world is a vivid reminder of God's promise of love, mercy, and forgiveness. A heavenly sign of hope, which Jean Kerr defined as "the feeling you have that the feeling you have is not permanent."

I like the story about the battered old man who got up one night during a revival meeting and said, "Brothers and sisters, you know and I know that I ain't been what I ought to have been. I've stolen hogs and told lies, and got drunk, and was always getting in fights, and shooting craps, and playing poker, and I've cussed and swore. But I thank the Lord there's one thing I ain't never done. I ain't ever lost my religion!"

On the brink of drowning in despair amidst a flood of temptation and sin, this neo-Noah never loses sight of God's rainbow of promise. That sacred vow, which Robert F. Capon graphically puts this way: "If you sin, God isn't going to do anything to you except die for you."

It is an obvious fact of life that we all have our apples, succumb to their seduction, and suffer the resultant physical and spiritual indigestion. Hopefully, it is just as evident that we all have our rainbows, God's gracious pledge that he loves us — no matter what. That is a promise that can buoy up the heaviest of hearts.

So watch out for the apples. And look up for the rainbows.

WHERE'S THE BEEF?

Tipping his soiled cowboy hat back on his head, propping his battered boots on the porch railing, B.V. (Beeves) Reeves leaned back in his old cowhide-bottomed rocker. He took a sip from his "Beef Is My Bread And Butter" coffee mug. As his scarred and calloused hands lowered his libation, twinkling eyes looked at me through the steam rising off the hot liquid, and a deep and raspy voice drawled, "Well, Ron, I figger if there was a tribe of Levis, that's a pretty good sign there were cowboys in early Bible times."

This conversation was getting more interesting by the moment.

It had all started when neighboring rancher Beeves and I got to talking about the apparent increase of those people who have a beef against beef.

For some it's a purely economic factor. As Beeves put it, "When you compare the price of beef and chicken, it's no wonder more and more people are biting the pullet!"

These people we can understand. The ones we both have a problem with are those vocal activists who are trying to convince the world that the basic cause of many of today's critical problems is cattle. Clogged human arteries, over-grazed public lands, the warming of the earth's atmosphere—all can be blamed on bovine beasts that put on too much mass, take in too much grass, and let out too much gas.

13

Even though we were both willing to admit that the cattle business is not without fault or above improvement, we also felt that much of the current criticism had gotten a little far-fetched and was fast approaching the ridiculous.

"I'm about ready to start quoting the Bible to those folks," Beeves said. "And a passage I'd like to start with is Psalm 50:9, 'I will accept no bull from your house!'" (RSV)

After smiling at Beeves' "inspired" interpretation of scripture, I mentioned my surprise at his knowledge of that verse.

That's when he informed me he had been doing some study of cattle in the Bible. Picking up a red Big Chief tablet from a shelf near his chair, Beeves began to share some of his findings.

"Cattle have been around from the very beginning," he said. "In Genesis 1:25 we read, 'God made...the cattle of every kind...And God saw that it was good.' (NRSV) If God made 'em and called 'em good, then cattle must not be all bad.

"And why did God make cattle? The same as everything else, as a gift to us human beings. In fact, Deuteronomy 7:13 says very point blank, God will love you and bless you 'with the increase of your cattle.' (RSV)

"I also find it interesting," he went on, "that wealth in those early nomadic tribes was measured in cattle. And there are some numbers mentioned that would impress even a Texas rancher. For example, in Numbers 31:33 Israel's booty from their victory in Midian included 72,000 oxen. King Hezekiah of Judah gave the assembly 1000 bulls for offerings (2 Chronicles 30:24.) And after Job went through all his trials, 'the Lord blessed his latter days more than his beginning.' And among his blessings were 1000 yoke of oxen (Job 42:12 RSV)."

Beeves paused to take another sip from his mug and flip through his notes. "Here's something I didn't know, Ron. In 2 Chronicles 4:4 it describes the temple altar as being built on 12 oxen, three facing each direction. That seems to me to place a pretty holy image on cattle."

Here I couldn't help but ask, "Speaking of biblical cattle images, how about the golden calf?"

"OK," Beeves admitted with a smile, "some of those ol' cattlemen did go overboard and tried to make a false god out of that golden calf. But don't forget the parable of the prodigal son and the 'fatted calf.' When the father barbecued that special calf for his son, it was a sign of love and forgiveness and celebration. Images don't get much better than that."

Putting his tablet back where he found it, Beeves looked at me with a wry grin and asked, "So, where's the beef?"

Laughing, I joined in with his rhetorical answer, "In the Bible, of course!"

"There," he said, leaning back in his rocker, "that ought to give those with a beef against beef something to put in their pot and chew on."

A Slip of the Tongue

When Pastor Forrest Kreinautlaud came to St. Martin's Lutheran Church in the mid-1980's, he soon discovered that the little Texas country church with its membership of predominately German-American farmers and ranchers was a bit behind its neighboring congregations in the practice of contemporary worship customs.

For example: other Lutheran congregations were involving more and more lay people in the worship. But not at St. Martin's. "That's the pastor's job," they said. "That's what we pay him for."

There was, however, one modern attitude toward worship at St. Martin's. That was the complaint about the length of the service, especially on communion Sundays.

In the old days they were in no hurry to leave church and go home. Dinner and nap could wait while they got their contributions worth out of worship and leisurely visited with their neighbors afterwards.

But that was in the days B.C.—Before Cowboys! Now that Dallas Cowboy professional football fever had caught on, they wanted to make sure there was plenty of time for them to get from their back pews in church to their front row seats before the TV sets.

So when Pastor Kreinautlaud pointed out that having lay people assist him with the distribution of the bread during communion would shorten the service on those Sundays, there was more openness to this new custom than usual. In fact, after only one "referral-to-committee," the church council adopted the proposal on a four-month trial basis — September through December.

Emil Aufderwahl was the obvious and unanimous choice to be the first communion assistant. Not only was he recognized as "the" lay leader of St. Martin's, but Emil also had another reputation that, in the eyes of many of his fellow members, qualified him for the job. That was his skill as a "Skat" player.

This traditional German game was still quite popular in the community, and Emil's talent at dealing the cards faster and more orderly than any one else around was admired by all. Though not spoken about during the church discussion, this ability was high in the minds of those who were thinking about speeding up the service. If Emil could deal cards quickly, he could do the same with thin communion wafers. This would cut down even more the time between the church benediction and Cowboy introductions.

So everything looked great for the successful implementation of something new into the long-time traditional worship customs of St. Martin's Lutheran Church.

But, alas, this was not to be. One of Emil Aufderwahl's little habits had been overlooked, one that was suddenly and glaringly apparent before he had completed distributing the wafers to the first group of worshippers who came and knelt before the altar.

Emil's fellow members had forgotten what it was that made him such a rapid dealer of cards. Their oversight was understandable, because what he did was quite socially acceptable at the card table, but shockingly offensive at the Lord's Table.

You see, Emil had this habit before he dealt each card of wetting his thumb with his tongue, a habit which he unconsciously brought with him to the church altar rail as he handed out each communion wafer!

Emil never realized what he was doing during the entire communion service. But the other members were very, very aware of what he was doing.

They were too German and too Lutheran, however, to do anything about it during the service. They just stoically accepted Emil's offering. Although more than one member later sheepishly admitted to faking eating the wafer and hiding it in their closed hand until a later secret disposal.

But right after the service, even though there was a Cowboy's kickoff just minutes away, an emergency church council meeting was called. By a unanimous vote the trial period for a communion assistant was immediately called to a halt.

And it was a long, long time before anyone ever mentioned changing St. Martin's traditional worship service again. The members never forgot that Sunday when they did try something new, and it had turned into a disaster—thanks to Emil Aufderwahl's slip-of-the-tongue.

Some Things Are Too Sacred
to Share

It was an Easter to remember.

The alarm rang at 2 A.M. After getting myself together, I joined our group for a long ride over a dusty, bumpy, high desert road to the remote Chama River Canyon area of Northern New Mexico. There at 4 A.M. we joined in worship at Christ in the Desert Benedictine Monastery.

For the next four hours I sat in the simple splendor of the adobe chapel with some 175 other early risers. In the darkness we listened to the traditional Easter Vigil readings accompanied by the ancient plainsong melodies for which monasteries are famous.

It was a mystical setting designed for meditation and contemplation. And I used it as such.

As I watched the sky through the high chapel windows, the stars slowly faded and the light of dawn gradually took their place. It was an unhurried time for me to reflect, not only on what was currently going on around me, but also to remember the events of the past week.

It all began on Palm Sunday as I joined fifteen people who had come from all across the country for a Holy Week retreat. The site was Ghost Ranch, the Presbyterian National Conference Center located about sixty miles northwest of Santa Fe.

On four previous visits I had discovered that a combination of high caliber programs and the scenic high desert setting makes Ghost Ranch a great place for "R & R," relaxation and reflection.

Sitting in the Easter service I thought back on the refreshing moments of silence and solitude I had enjoyed roaming the secluded canyons and mesas of the 21,000-acre ranch.

There were also meaningful times of community with my fellow retreaters. Daily study and worship had quickly brought us together as a family. Our bond had been further strengthened as we shared the experiences of encountering some of the unique spiritual traditions associated with Holy Week in Northern New Mexico.

On Holy Thursday evening we had journeyed to the nearby village of Abiquiu. There we joined the local community in a service of foot washing. Good Friday morning we walked eight miles as a part of the pilgrimage to the Santuario de Chimayo. That afternoon we were privileged to return to Abiquiu and observe the little seen Stations-of-the-Cross ceremony led by Los Hermanos. Also known as Penitentes, this formerly secret group of village laymen welcomed our presence as brothers and sisters in the family of Christ.

All the wondrous happenings of the past week were fresh on my mind as I sat in the monastery chapel. Processing these thoughts, the question naturally arose, "What now? How will this experience affect my life after the retreat is over? How will I share what has happened to me this week with those who were not here?"

I came to no satisfactory answer until after the service was over and our group had gathered for the retreat closure.

As if reading my mind, our leader reminded us of Mark's Gospel account of the Easter events. The women left their encounter with the angel and the empty tomb and "said nothing to anyone, because they were afraid."

What the women had experienced was so awesome, so mysterious and their reaction so personal that there was no way they could share what had happened with those who had not been there.

Their fear was of mis-communicating. How could they tell others what they had seen, heard and felt—when they themselves didn't fully understand what they had experienced?

The Easter events were something the women needed to ponder in their hearts, as Mary had done after the remarkable events surrounding Jesus' birth.

Just so, our Holy Week retreat experiences were not something we should attempt to share too quickly with others. Mull it over for awhile. Cogitate upon it. Mediate. Contemplate. Reflect. Ponder.

We had been to the mountaintop. And we would do well to remember the reaction of those who were witnesses to the amazing happenings on the biblical Mount of Transfiguration, "The disciples kept quiet about all this and told no one at that time anything they had seen." (Luke 9:36 GNB)

Some things are too sacred to share!

Of all the things I experienced during the Ghost Ranch retreat—that just may be the most profound. It is definitely something I continue to ponder in my heart.

JUST HANG LOOSE!

A city slicker went on his first deer hunt. One morning he came back to camp with his camo clothes in tatters, face and arms covered with scratches and bruises. He looked like he'd caught on fire and somebody had tried to put him out with a weed-whacker!

When his buddies saw him they asked, "What in the world happened to you?"

"A big black snake chased me," replied the novice outdoorsman.

"But a black snake isn't poisonous," one of the experienced hunters pointed out.

"Listen," said the city guy, "if he can make me jump off a forty-foot cliff, he doesn't have to be!"

That story would seem to confirm the observation of the late Senator Sam Ervin, "The world is full of people who go through life running from something that isn't chasing them."

One of those "black snakes" is worry, which Larry Winget defines as "simply the misuse of the imagination."

A pastor was preaching on worry. To emphasize the importance of not worrying, he assured the congregation that "ninety percent of the time, those things we worry about never happen."

"So," came a self-satisfied voice from the back of the church, "it works!"

Evidently a lot of people agree with that wit in the pew because there is a mess of worrying going on. I know. I've done my share of it.

In my years as a worrier warrior I've learned a couple of things.

One is the truth of comedienne Judy Tenuta's line, "Worry is having more confidence in your problems than in a cosmic power to solve them."

In a sense, worry is atheism. It dethrones God and puts us in his place. We become "the captains of our fate, the masters of our soul." All the pressure and responsibility of living falls on our shoulders, a load not even the strongest of humans can carry.

To relieve that burden I need to be constantly reminded that I am not God—God is. And then remember what the Gospel tells me about who God is: all-powerful creator, loving saviour, and ever-present spirit.

Being human, however, there are times when, wrestling with a passel of hassles, I forget all that, and worry worms its way back. That is when Thomas Merton's advice comes in handy, "God does not ask you not to feel anxious, but to trust in him no matter how you feel."

The second thing I've learned, Kennon Callahan says better than I: "When you worry, worry over a worry worth worrying about. Worry about something worthwhile. Worry over something you can do something about. Then having worried in a worthwhile way—RELAX!"

On a trip to Hawaii I heard a phrase that seems to be the unofficial state motto, "Hang Loose!" Our tour guides reminded us over and over again,

"You're on vacation. Enjoy yourself. Relax. Take it easy. Just hang loose!"

A great antidote for worry is to take a vacation, which someone has described as, "what you take when you can no longer take what you've been taking all along."

The biblical teachings about the Sabbath pointedly emphasize the importance of rest. Our bodies need it, as well as our souls and mind. I have found that nothing frees me from the restlessness of worry better than some restful, enjoyable distraction.

So whenever I get all wound up and uptight with my hang ups, I know it's time to unwind, take it easy, and "just hang loose!"

Isaiah sums up what I have learned about dealing with the woes of worry this way, "In returning and rest you shall be saved; in quietness and trust shall be your strength." (30:15 RSV)

Or as they might put it in Hawaii, "Hang loose and you'll hang tough."

EXPECTING THE UNEXPECTED

"What a revoltin' development this is!"

Chester A. Riley's classic exclamation from the days of early radio came to mind while a posthole was being dug in our ranch pens. About a foot into the hole, water began to spew into the air. An artesian well? No. A busted PVC pipe!

My dad had put the pipes in for the water troughs. I was not around at the time, but I thought I knew where they were, and we had been very careful while digging in those areas. This pipe, however, was not where I supposed it to be. Its eruption came as a total surprise.

(One moral of this story is: There should be a law that no rancher can die until he has left for following generations a map of everything that is underground.)

Running to the reservoir, the digger turned over a rock where the cut-off valve was supposed to be, only to discover it was the wrong rock. No cut-off —but there was one disturbed little button rattle-snake!

Disposing of the snake, the digger decided he'd rather go looking for a coupling in the tool shed than turn over more rocks. He found several of those—all the wrong size! So jumping into the pickup, he raced seven miles to another source, got the right repair piece, sped back to the pens, waded into the water, bridged the broken gap with the coupling, and collapsed on the ground, a weary, wet and wiser man.

Expecting the unexpected is a part of ranch life. Trees fall on fences. Livestock get out. Fire ants short out a water pump. You name a negative possibility and you can positively expect it to become a probability.

Fortunately, the opposite is also true. These unexpected experiences can often be positive instead of negative; good, not bad; bringers of smiles instead of snarls.

For example: while digging in our pens on another occasion, I unearthed a 1925 car license plate, a buried treasure from my granddad's era. Or there have been those dry times when non-forecasted rain came out of the blue. Or the warehouse where our mohair was stored calling to say somebody wanted to buy it—at a decent price!

Not all the surprises of ranching are downers. Many of the unforeseen events can lift the spirits, lighten the load, and brighten the gloom. These are the times when the rancher tilts his hat back, looks to the skies, and says, "This ol' way of life ain't so bad after all. I might just keep on doin' it a little while longer."

Expecting the unexpected is a part of my workaday life. And my spiritual life, as well.

For the biblical disciples, life with Jesus was one unexpected experience after another. But he saved the biggest surprise for last.

Still stunned by the startling crucifixion of Jesus on Friday—which they must have regarded as the ultimate "revoltin' development"—the dejected disciples trudged to his tomb on Sunday morning, not knowing they were about to encounter one more unexpected event, the penultimate revitalizing development of Jesus' resurrection.

They came to say "Goodbye" to Jesus.
Instead, he said "Hello" to them!
They arrived to play "Taps" for a dead leader.
Instead their living Lord played "Reveille" for them!
They went to the grave thinking it was all over.
Instead they discovered it was just beginning!
They gathered to mourn a death.
Instead they departed rejoicing in life!

In my own encounters with the Christ there have been no occurrences quite as dramatic as those of the disciples. I have, however, had my share of unexpected eye-opening revelations.

Times when I expected the wrath of God,
but instead received his grace!
Moments when I expected rejection,
but instead received acceptance!
Occasions when I thought it was all over.
but instead received a second chance!

All of these unforeseen experiences have given me great respect and reverence for my surprising God—and the excitement of living in eager expectation of the unexpected!

FEETNOTES

Coming out of the La Villita Assembly Hall in San Antonio who should I see sitting on a bench with his shoes off, rubbing his feet, but old friend Tex Luther.

Walking over to him I asked, "What are you doing?"

With a sly grin he looked up and replied, "I'm sitting here envying the Israelites in the wilderness."

"How's that?"

"In Deuteronomy Moses reminded the people of Israel how God took care of them on their exodus trek, 'The clothes on your back did not wear out and your feet did not swell those forty years.' (8:5 NRSV)

"Just think of that, Ron. Forty years of walking in a desert full of hot sand, stones, stickers—and no foot problems! While here I am, not even forty hours into this Pastor's Conference, and my feet are killing me! That's why I envy the Israelites."

Laughing, I sat down beside him. "I know what you mean," I said, kicking off my shoes. "My old dogs are beginning to bark, too. I've been so busy roaming around talking to people, I think this is the first time I've sat down in the last four hours."

"Me too," said Tex. "My problem when I come to events like this is to take Martin Luther literally, 'Here I stand!' But instead of 'standing on the promises,' I find myself 'standing on the *premises*.' And my feet pay the penalty."

That comment jogged my memory. "At one of the first gatherings like this I attended after my ordination, a veteran foot-soldier in the clergy corps gave me this advice: 'Ron, if you're going to survive the ministry, never miss a chance to rest your feet.' You'd think after all these years I'd learn to do that."

"Yeah, I got a lot of wise counsel when I was a rookie reverend myself," said Tex. "And it seems like the only one I've paid any attention to is, 'Keep both feet on the ground.'"

The conversation paused as we both massaged our tootsies. Then I said, "Listen to us. Here we are, men of the soul and spirit, at a conference to sharpen our minds and hone our professional skills, and what are we concerned about? Our feet!"

"Well now, that may not be as out of place as you think it is," said Tex, turning thoughtful. "The Bible has a bunch of references to foot care. Weary travelers welcomed by having their feet cleansed. Jesus washing Peter's feet. The woman bathing Jesus' feet with her tears. The implication being that service to other people and reverence for Jesus is shown by caring for their feet."

"And another thing we often overlook," said Tex, "is the respect those Biblical people had for Jesus' feet. For example, the women at the tomb encounter the risen Jesus and, as Matthew says, they 'took hold of his feet, and worshipped him.' (28:9 GNB) I believe that ties in to the passage in Roman where Paul quotes Isaiah, 'How beautiful are the feet of those who bring good news!' (10:15 NRSV) Those women realized they never would have heard the message of peace and salvation from the lips of Jesus, never felt the healing touch of his hand, if his feet hadn't carried him to them first. They knew how important those human feet that trod the sod of earth were in connecting them with God and heaven."

There was silence as Tex's words sunk in. Then I asked him, "Do you agree with Luther's statement, 'Each Christian is a little Christ?'"

"I sure do."

"Then you realize the implication of what you're saying."

"Right. Christ's feet are my feet. Your feet. Every Christian's feet."

We both thought about that a minute. Then Tex leaned back on his elbows, lifted his feet up in the air, and said, "These ol' feet do get tired and sore and achy sometimes," and here he paused to give his toes a jaunty wiggle, "but aren't they beautiful!"

Breaking the Sound Barrier

I was proud of my new ranch bedroom clock. Push a bottom and the digital numbers lit up in the dark of night, big and bright enough that even without my glasses I could read them.

The only problem was—the alarm didn't work. But I figured I could live with that small defect. After all when you have reached the age when you normally arise in time to wake the rooster, an alarm is seldom, if ever, needed.

It was several weeks before my wife had the opportunity to visit the ranch for an overnight stay. In the early morning hours I awoke to see her leaning over me pointing toward the clock on my side of the bed. Punching the illuminator button, I squinted, then proudly proclaimed, "It's 5 o'clock."

"I know what *time* it is," replied an uncharacteristically aggravated Alberta. "Turn off the *alarm!*"

"What alarm?" I innocently asked.

"THE ONE THAT'S BEEN BUZZING FOR THE LAST FIVE MINUTES!!!"

With that incident I added another item to the list of things not on my aging ear's wavelength.

A recent hearing test had revealed that a combination of time, genetics and exposure to loud noises had taken its toll. Certain sounds enter the lobby of my ear, but find the receptionist "out-to-lunch." As a result, my brain back in the office never gets the message.

Leading the list of unacknowledged visitors are modern electronic devices such as alarm clocks, cordless telephones and automobile turn signals. But some human voices make the roster as well, notably certain women and children.

When I discussed this problem with my family physician, he responded with a wry smile, "Don't worry about it. This is God's gift to aging men."

I must admit there are some positive possibilities to hearing loss. Like during stormy nights in our tin-roofed ranch house when I can put my good ear down in the pillow, my bad ear up, and sleep right through the whole thing.

There have even been pleasant pluses in my marital relationship. Alberta and I, for instance, still sit close together in the car when we travel. Just like we did when we were young. The only difference being that back then we sat close because we were young and freshly and madly in love. Now we sit close so we can hear each other!

So there are "pros" to being "aurally inconvenienced" (the politically correct term). However, there are "cons" as well.

I can do without the noise, but not without the music; without the clock alarm, but not the fire alarm; without the telemarketing call, but not the family call.

There are certain things I want to hear, I need to hear. One of those definitely being the voice of God.

On numerous occasions Jesus said, "He who has ears to hear, let him hear." But what about those of us "who have ears to hear, but hear not?" We who drive with our blinkers on, who sleep through alarms, whose prime contribution to many a conversation is, "Huh?" Are we not on God's wavelength?

Fortunately for us Jesus was not speaking literally. He knew that sound relations are not always dependent upon sounds. Hearing another has just as much to do with the heart as with the ears.

I don't have to hear the words to get the message. Just because I'm deaf does not mean I'm dumb or numb. I still have enough sense and working senses that I can pick up the signals others are sending.

I may not always catch the words from God, from family, from friends. But I hear the message. The good news that I am loved, failing ears and all. Love breaks the sound barrier.

My response? To joyfully shout, "HEAR! HEAR!"

THE PROS OF PROCRASTINATION

For years I have been meaning to write on procrastination. But I just kept putting it off.

This says something about my personality. I am a pro-crastinator. There is nothing amateur about my "crastinating" at all. My proclivity and proficiency for procrastination is a proven factor. In fact, I have risen to the advanced level of the practitioners of procrastination who believe with Mark Twain, "Never put off till tomorrow what you can put off till the day *after* tomorrow."

I fit all the descriptions of a procrastinator. I am a person with a *wait* problem. I am someone who won't take *now* for an answer. And I suffer from the disease "hardening of the oughteries."

We live in a "Do It Now!" world. We are bombarded by old sayings like: "He who hesitates is lost." "Time waits for no man." And, "Procrastination is the thief of time."

As one who does not live up to these supposedly wise words of advice, I have felt my share of guilt. Herb True's little poem describes me exactly:

"Procrastination is my sin.
It brings me naught but sorrow.
I know that I should stop it.
In fact, I will—tomorrow!"

Lately, however, I have begun to realize that among all of the "cons," there are also some "pros" in procrastination.

For example, the old proverb, "Look before you leap," warns us of the danger of acting too hastily.

"Never do today what you can do as well to-morrow," advised Aaron Burr. "Delay may give clearer light as to what is best to be done." Thomas Jefferson gave the same wise counsel when he said, "Delay is preferable to error." And some contemporary wit has put it in my kind of language, "Sometimes it's better to put off until tomorrow what you are likely to make a mess of today."

There is even a Biblical passage that underscores this way of thinking: "One who moves too hurriedly misses the way." (Proverbs 19:2 NRSV)

All of which leads me to what might be the strongest "pro" in procrastination:

"If you want to keep from trouble
Here's a mighty easy way:
Always put off till tomorrow
What you shouldn't do today." (Anonymous)

Instead of thinking of procrastination as a sin, maybe we should look at it as a protection against sin.

For instance: dragging your feet can be a good thing when trying to resist the pull of temptation. Burning with lust? Put your passion on ice. So mad you want to kill somebody? Kill time instead. In short, to prevent a sinful fall, stall.

Such tabling of emotions, of putting off questionable actions until tomorrow, can often put off a lot of sorrow until tomorrow as well. And when that happens, procrastination becomes a positive, desirable virtue. As someone has said, "It's better to sleep on what you plan to do than be kept awake by what you have done."

So instead of protesting and prosecuting procrastination as a problem to be prohibited, I propose a program to proudly proclaim, promote and produce the profound promises, the profuse prospects, the productive profits provided with the prudent practice of procrastination.

If you would like to help out in this project, just give me a holler—tomorrow!

WILL THERE BE ANY MAALOX ™ IN HEAVEN?

"Extra Strength Maalox™." The black lettering on the clear wrapper was repeated three times, leaving no doubt as to the contents. The individual packet was torn and empty now. The tablet used, the container discarded.

Millions of these little packages are used and thrown away each day, I'm sure. But this was the first one I had ever found in a hunting blind on our ranch!

Oh, I've found lots of other things left behind by hunters. Candy and gum wrappers, Kleenex, toothpicks, empty pecan hulls, spent shell casings. Sometimes even more substantial leavings forgotten in the excitement of the hunt—binoculars, flashlights, knives, caps. But antacid wrappers? Never before.

I must admit I was offended by my discovery. Not that it was litter (Outside the blind I would have been upset; inside I can clean it up before it scatters.) I was affronted that there had been the need for such a potion on our "happy hunting ground!"

Maalox™ has become a symbol of all the stress, tension, and anxiety that fills our hectic world. I like to think that our ranch is a place to escape from all that. A serene, relaxed, haven of peace and quiet. A refuge to ease the acid, calm the colon, and mend the mind.

At least it has been that for me. If I had not been able to escape to this personal Garden of Eden over the years, I would not have survived mentally, physically, emotionally, or spiritually.

And that is one of the main reasons I share this place. So that others can experience the same healing.

My problem, however, is a tendency to forget that such healing does not take place overnight. Storms may calm instantaneously in Biblical miracles, but in modern everyday life it usually takes a little longer for the wind and the waves to subside.

People don't drive into our ranch and receive immediate peace and tranquility. The entrance to "The Red Hill" is not the golden gate to heaven. Just a rusty gate to a heavenly place.

All kinds of hunters came through that entrance this particular season—over fifteen during the first month. I have no idea who brought the Maalox™. Chances are more than one of these visitors had such medication in their gear.

And for good reason.

Many of these people came here to get away from professional pressures.

Pastors of congregations in conflict. An administrator of a multi-million dollar statewide agency. A Dallas policeman. A professor on a university campus torn by strife over an unpopular president. A Seattle anesthetist. People considering moves they really did not want to make. Others wanting to change professional positions and no opportunities. All reasons for an occasional Maalox™ or two.

And there were also problems of a personal nature.

Health problems were common among visitors. One hunter had two heart attacks in the spring. Another had back surgery in August. And still another had hernia surgery less than a month before he came to the ranch.

Then there were family problems. A third of my guests had been divorced. All had remarried except one, and his wedding was scheduled within a month. Some of those who had not been divorced had marriages that were a little shaky.

Children made their contribution to the anxiety. College age students needing financial support. Teenagers going through that tough transition time from dependent child to independent adult. One guy in his fifties with a second family of two boys under seven—plus an eighteen-month-old foster child!

No wonder my visitors needed a little help in tablet form!

The more I thought about it, the less I was offended by my hunting blind discovery. I began to understand the plight of my guests, as well as my role as their host.

If I am to provide an environment of healing hospitality, it means my task is to pick up the empty Maalox™ wrappers—and keep the gate open!

St. Gallo's or St. Shiner's?

"I'm thinking of changing the name of our church to St. Gallo's," mused fellow pastor Tex Luther over coffee.

"Why's that?" I asked.

"Because sometimes I feel like I'm working in a *whinery*," he answered with a grim smile.

"My office has become the complaint department at our church. I am besieged by *'groan-ups,'* people who seem to think that the basic rule of church life is, 'For every action there is an equal and opposite criticism.'"

"Sounds to me like you've discovered the truth of that old one-liner, 'Not everyone up in the air and harping on something is an angel,'" I said.

"Boy, you can say that again," he quickly responded. "It's gotten so I can't even sing 'Home on the Range' without changing the line to say, 'where never is heard an *encouraging* word.'"

After taking a sip from his cup, Tex went on. "My one consolation is that this is nothing new. I roamed through my concordance the other day and rediscovered several biblical passages addressing the same problem.

"For example: Jude 1:16, 'These people are always grumbling and blaming others.' And James 5:9, 'Do not complain against one another.' Even Jesus had to deal with a similar situation when in John 6:43 he says, 'Stop grumbling among yourselves.' Or the translation I prefer, by Clarence Jordan, 'Quit your bellyaching!'"(GNB)

"Looks to me like you've got the texts for a sermon you might need to preach," I commented.

"I've thought about that," Tex said. "And the one I'm going to use is Philippians 2:14: 'Do everything without complaining or arguing...shine...like stars lighting up the sky.'" (GNB)

"Going to accentuate the positive, huh?"

"Right. I'm going to ask, 'Who do you like to be around? Someone who makes you feel bad? Or someone who makes you feel good? A discourager or an encourager? A whiner or a shiner?'

"People are not attracted to a dark and gloomy church filled with frowning, grumbling, whining, bellyaching gripers. But a bright and shining church of smiling, cheerful, complimentary, appreciative encouragers—that is attractive and appealing.

"Winston Churchill once said of Franklin Roosevelt, 'Meeting him was like opening a bottle of champagne!' Wouldn't it be great if people could say that about Christians?

"In that list of gifts in Romans 12, the Good New Bible translation of verse 8 is the gift 'to encourage others.' That is something for which all Christians need to pray. The insight to look for the best in others, not the worst. The talent to hearten our fellow humans not dishearten them. The gift of building people up, not tearing them down.

"Nothing can lift an individual out of depression and make life a joy more than being appreciated. Nothing can build up a congregation's spirits and make it attractive to others more than a positive, affirming, encouraging environment.

"And how do we do that? By taking seriously that biblical exhortation, 'Do everything without complaining or arguing…shine…like stars lighting up the sky.'"

Ending his sermon rehearsal, Tex leaned back and looked at me with an expression of, "Well, what do you think?"

With a smile of approval I said, "Preach that, Tex, and instead of 'St. Gallo's,' maybe you can rename your church 'St. Shiner's!'"

A Farewell Party

Life is full of little ironies. One of these occurred for me on Friday, October 2, 1992.

On that day I spoke at the funeral of my uncle, Jack Williams. It was held in the Little Church of the Flowers at Forest Lawn Cemetery, Glendale, California.

Uncle Jack was born in San Antonio, Texas. He moved to Southern California when he was sixteen and ended up spending most of his life in the Los Angeles area.

I currently live near San Antonio and have spent most of my life in Texas. I like to think of myself as a native Texan. When asked "place of birth," however, I must reply, Glendale, California!

Irony of ironies: I had come from the place of Uncle Jack's birth, to the city of my birth, to speak at his funeral.

Ironic though the circumstances were, it all seemed strangely fitting. As Uncle Jack and I were connected at his death, so we were also connected at my birth.

Jack and his oldest brother, Homer, along with their sister, Bess, and her husband, Willis Birk (my parents), all went to California in the 1920's. They had gone in search of the pot of gold at the rainbow's end of the west coast.

Shortly after they arrived, however, they discovered the rusty reality of "The Depression."

Uncle Jack moved in with my parents and for some seven years the three pooled their resources against the harsh economic deprivations of those hard times.

It was during those years that I was born. The first nuclear family I ever experienced had my uncle as an intimate, integral part of it.

Even though my parents moved back to Texas when I was five and most of our contact for the next 52 years was long distance, Uncle Jack and I still had a surprisingly close relationship.

Letters, phone calls, periodic visits—in all these ways we kept in touch. And in spite of all those years and miles, we managed to maintain a deep feeling of family.

Just six months before his death we had had a celebration of that family. Uncle Jack's son had brought him back to Texas for a visit. And on Sunday, April 12, 1992, six of the eight of we Williams of my generation gathered to honor the last of the Williams from the previous generation. It was Uncle Jack's 82nd birthday.

Gathered in the old rock house on our ranch, we Williams from Texas and California had a ball. We laughed. We hugged. We shared old photos and all the memories that went with them.

Sitting in the middle of all this, with a big grin under his silly little paper birthday hat, was Uncle Jack soaking up all that familiar warmth.

Finally after "Happy Birthday" was sung, after the cake was eaten, after the humorous cards and gag gifts were presented, we started sharing tributes to our family patriarch.

It soon became clear that here was a man dearly loved by us all. His lifelong playful spirit, his abiding sense of humor, his cheerful outlook on a life that had not always treated him kindly, his obvious care and respect for all of us gathered there—in our eyes those attributes combined to make Uncle Jack, by unanimous vote, "Favorite Uncle of His Generation."

Afterwards, if he told me once, he told me a dozen times, "Ronald, that was the greatest day of my life!"

I'm sure that evaluation was an exaggeration on his part, but it did communicate his deep appreciation for this family gathering and the outpouring of warmth and support towards him.

This was especially meaningful to my uncle in light of the fact that just a few weeks before, after the trip to Texas and the party had already been planned, he had learned of his cancer. On the day after he returned to California, he began his chemotherapy.

We did something good and caring and loving at that birthday party, which all of us knew subconsciously was also a going-away party.

Who knows how comforting that outpouring of affection was to Uncle Jack during the ensuing months of pain? Who knows how much he was warmed by the knowledge that he was the "Favorite Uncle" of a widely scattered yet still close and caring family?

When that farewell day came to an end, I believe Uncle Jack realized what the Psalmist meant when he said, "God setteth the solitary in families." And I like to think that knowledge fared him well right up to the end of his life.

SIZABLE SHORTS, SOFT SOLES, SPIRITUAL SERENITY AND OTHER COMFORTS OF OLD AGE

"I went to a men's store and asked for three pairs of Jockey shorts.

'What size, sir?' said the clerk.

'Thirty-four,' I replied.

'Would you like them gift wrapped?' he said."

That story told by Bill Cosby in his book *Time Flies* (Doubleday, New York, 1987) is accompanied by this commentary:

"It is a point of pride for the American male to keep the same size Jockey shorts for his entire life. He can lose his house in a crap game and his wife to the mailman, but his ego cannot tolerate an increase in his Jockey short size: and so, you have a man with a brand-new 40-inch waist who is trying to get into size 36 Jockey shorts, a man who is now wearing a combination of supporter and tourniquet. Proud men in their thirties and forties have gone to the brink of gangrene to maintain the interior fashion of their youth."

I can identify with Cosby's observation. After twenty years of wearing the same size undershorts, I realized that one size larger was much more comfortable.

Like it or not, I am seeing subtle little signs that this 1935-model human being is beginning to show the mileage of the years.

For example: the humor of a "Born Loser" cartoon hits close to home. It shows a man walking up behind his wife sitting in a chair and commenting, "Oh, ho! And what is this I see? Someone has a lot of snow on the old roof."

The wife's comment is, "At least someone's shingles haven't all fallen out!"

Not only is my hair turning gray, it is also turning loose!

There are other indications that the AARP membership card in my wallet is not out of place.

Such as, being tempted to order items in catalogs that I never even noticed in my younger years. These include: devices to increase the volume on phones and TVs; "Happy Feet" cushioned insoles; "Ear Loks" that keep ones eyeglasses from slipping: "Trim and Slim Body Control Shirts," nostrums for hemorrhoid and intestinal gas relief, and, oh shame of it all, nose hair clippers!

Even an old Bible passage has begun to be meaningful:

> "So remember your Creator while you are still young, before those dismal days and years come when you will say, 'I don't enjoy life.' That is when the light of the sun, the moon, and the stars will grow dim for you, and the rain clouds will never pass away. Then your arms, that have protected you, will tremble, and your legs, now strong, will grow weak. Your teeth will be too few to chew your food, and your eyes too dim to see clearly. Your ears will be deaf to the noise of the street. You will barely be able to hear the mill as it grinds or

music as it plays, but even the song of a bird will wake you from sleep. You will be afraid of high places, and walking will be dangerous. Your hair will turn white; you will hardly be able to drag yourself along, and all desire will be gone." (Ecclesiastes 12:1-5. *Good News Bible*)

Yes, as the biblical writer describes so vividly, old age has its physical downside. But I have not come to that point where I will say, "I don't enjoy life." I have become aware that there is an up-side to these years as well.

I may not be as sleek and as firm as I once was. My eyes and ears may miss things they used to pick up easily. The number of my hairs may be less, and my digestive system not as hospitable to certain things that pass through it as in younger years.

But when it comes to mental sagacity, emotional security, and spiritual serenity, I am sooooo much better off than when I was young that it all evens out.

Old age or youth? Both have their strong and weak points. I enjoyed my youth, and I am enjoying my older years. That just may be the sign of a balanced, good life. And for that, I am thankful!

A World of Difference

One thing we all have in common is—we are all different!

Few truths in life are more obvious. Every time we encounter another person we are reminded that human beings are not uniform stamped-out products of some heavenly assembly line. Each of us is a hand-crafted original, uniquely designed, custom made by the Creator.

We all have distinctive physical characteristics. We each have one-of-a-kind personalities. People don't look alike. They don't look at life alike. We vary greatly in our appearances, our attitudes, our actions.

Along with the fact that we are all different, another thing we all have in common is difficulty in dealing with our differences.

It may be obvious we are different from each other, but it is just as obvious that we have trouble accepting these differences.

Most wars are fought between groups that regard each other as "different." Different countries, different races, different political philosophies, and, sadly, even different religions.

Most personal "wars," the conflicts between individuals, have the same root cause—the differences between us. Different looks, different languages, and different lifestyles—you name the difference, and somewhere, sometime, two people have locked horns over it.

Differences between people can cause difficulties between people.

This is the issue Paul addresses in the 12th chapter of his first letter to the church in Corinth where opposing factions threaten to split the church. He stresses that unity in the church does not mean uniformity among church members.

Just as a healthy body has many different parts, so does the "body of Christ." Each part has different gifts, different functions. But the common goal of all these various parts is the same – to work together for the good of the whole body.

This means that instead of looking at people who are different from us as threats to us, we now see them as complements to us. Our differences don't divide us; they bring us together. Instead of taking up arms against those who are different, we now join arms with them. Instead of going to war against each other, we go to work with each other.

As members of the body of Christ, our unity is not in our uniformity; our unity is really in our diversity.

I like the way Gerald Mann puts it: "Christians are brothers and sisters in the family of God. But not *twin* brothers and sisters!"

All Christians are *not* identical. They don't look alike, think alike, or act alike. But they can still live together, love together—each using their special gifts, their unique talents, for the good of the whole family.

As the cartoon character Ziggy says, "Many of us are more capable than some of us—but none of us is as capable as *all* of us!!"

The point of all this? Very simply: WE NEED EACH OTHER!

With all our differences, with all our difficulties in dealing with these differences, I still need you. And you need me.

In a world of differences, we need each other. And when we work together, it can make a world of difference.

Getting a Handle on God

"The ark of the covenant had handles."

That was the rather surprising answer I got from pastoral buddy Tex Luther when I asked him what his sermon had been about the previous Sunday.

The subject of our casual coffee conversation concerned his congregation and its annual fruit-basket-turnover of members. "When you're located in a city with a large university, a major military base, and several sizeable national corporations," Tex explained, "you learn to expect and accept such constant comings and going."

"But it still must be a tough place to do ministry," I said.

"I'll admit there are times when I feel like the Chaplain at DFW Airport," he replied. "However, I have found it to be an exciting opportunity to remind people of a basic truth about God. It is something I do in individual conversations the year round and in a sermon, which I re-run every summer to the entire worshipping community. In fact, I used it just last Sunday."

That was when I asked him what the sermon was about and received the answer, "The ark of the covenant had handles."

My curiosity was aroused. "Please, tell me more."

Tex was only too glad to do so. "When I first came here, I was trying to figure out how to pastor a bunch of people who 'all seem to have tumbleweed blood in our veins,' as one of them from West Texas put it. I found the answer while reading Harvey Cox's *The Secular City* (The Macmillan Company, New York, 1965). Remember that?"

"You bet. *The* theological book of the sixties. Must reading for any 'with it' Pastor."

"Right. A section of the book deals with the mobility of modern society and its effect upon the church. Cox acknowledges the negative threats, but then points out the positive possibilities. He does that by reminding us that Yahweh, the Old Testament God, was a mobile God. The Jews were nomads. And so was their God. Yahweh was not tied down, as were the 'baals,' the immobile gods of certain towns and places. Where the Jews went, Yahweh went, too."

"And the ark of the covenant," I said, catching his drift, "was the symbol of that mobility."

"Yes," said Tex. "Basically the ark was meant to be a reminder of God's presence with his people. But the rings on the side, with the carrying poles inserted through them and the specific instructions that 'the poles are to be left in the rings and must never be taken out,' that added a unique twist to the symbol. Yahweh was a portable God. A God who could be picked up and carried with his people whenever they moved from one place to another."

"Cox concludes that this was a revolutionary new view of God, which had enormous theological significance," Tex went on. "It meant Yahweh could not be limited to, or localized at, any given geographical spot. This was a God who traveled with his people. And the idea of a footloose, rambling, gadabout God was radically different from that of the baals, stick-in-the-mud homebodies who stayed put in one place. Yahweh could be anyplace, anytime, anyhow."

"And the significance of that for today's mobile society?" I asked.

With a smile, Tex said, "I don't think God has settled down yet. We may be a people on the go. But so is God. We never need to be afraid of going to some 'God-forsaken place.' God is always with us, wherever we are. The carrying poles have not been taken out. The ark of the covenant of his presence still has its handles."

Don't Go Barefoot to a Snake Stompin'!

(During 20 years as a campus pastor, I was never invited to speak at a university graduation ceremony. If I had been asked, however, I would have included some of the following remarks.)

The man had taken a picture to an art shop for framing. At the counter he heard the woman in front of him tell the sales clerk that she wanted a frame for a $20,000 picture.

The clerk gasped and stammered that although the shop did not usually handle such expensive items, they would certainly do their best.

The woman nodded and lay on the counter her son's college diploma!

Some wit has commented that Graduation Day has a special meaning to parents. It means "The Bucks Stop Here!"

No question about it, a college education today costs a lot of money. However, as Derek Bok observed, "If you think education is expensive, try ignorance."

There is an old English proverb that says, "Stupidity won't kill you—but it sure can make you sweat!"

You can get by today without a higher education, but chances are you will sweat a lot less if you have it.

"Don't go barefoot to a snake stompin'" is an old Texas saying. The world out there is full of all kinds of "snakes." To make it you need all the protection, all the ammunition, you can get.

College is an excellent place to "put your boots on," to prepare yourself to battle the serpents that lie in wait along your pathway through life.

Wise people have witnessed to the importance of education in that battle.

"Education makes life easier. For instance, if you hadn't learned to sign your name, you'd have to pay cash for everything." (Anonymous)

"College is the key to success in later life," says Robert Orben, "because all students learn something that will be critically important to them in the business world—how to sit and pretend to listen for 50 minutes at a time."

"A degree from a good college prepares you to say, 'That's not my area of expertise,' instead of 'I don't know.'" (Ivern Ball)

And one of the wisest observations of all comes from Robert Frost, "Education is the ability to listen to almost anything without losing your temper or your self-confidence."

Self esteem is so important in life. Another of America's famous poets, Muhammad Ali, gave this good advice to a group of inner-city students:

"Stay in college.
Get the knowledge.
Stay there till you're through.
If they can make penicillin out of moldy bread,
They can sure make something out of you."

Education helps you learn who you are—that you are somebody. And that knowledge can take much of the fear out of life.

A young skater was having a bad case of butterflies before an event. She told her coach she was just too afraid to go out on the ice.

"You're not afraid. You're just nervous," said the coach. "There's a difference."

He explained it this way: a man goes into a restaurant and orders a $100 meal. He's nervous because he ordered such a high-priced meal, but he knows he has the $100 in his pocket.

"Now fear," said the coach, "is going into a restaurant and ordering a $100 meal, knowing you have *no money in your pocket.*"

The skater went out and finished first in the competition.

As you face all the risks of life ahead of you, it's OK to be nervous, but you don't have to be afraid. Why? Because you have something in your pocket. You have your education. And that will pay for some pretty high-priced meals.

Bill Cosby has written, "There are those who graduate *Cum Laude*. Those who graduate *Summa Cum Laude*. And those who graduate "Thank You Laude."

Be thankful for your education.

"Happy is the man who becomes wise—who comes to have understanding. There is more profit in it than there is in silver; it is more to you than gold. Wisdom is more valuable than jewels; nothing you could want can compare with it. Wisdom offers you long life, as well as wealth and honor. Wisdom can make your life pleasant and lead you safely through it. Those who become wise are happy: wisdom will give them life." (Proverbs 3:13-18 GNB)

LIFE IS LOUD!

The child was showing off his newly learned talking skills. When the words failed to come, he filled in with drinking-glass-shattering screeches. Fortunately the airline was using plastic containers. Unfortunately my eardrums, separated from the prospective horror movie star by only a thin seat back, were made of flesh.

Off the plane. Into a motel room. But still no rest for weary ears. The pool was close enough that the rowdy revelry of swimmers wafted in until 11:30 P.M. Even silent sleep, when it finally came, was not immune. My eyes popped open at 5 A.M., rudely unlatched by snoring snorts. Since I was alone in my room, it took a while to determine the source— an occupant of the bed only inches away on the other side of the obviously un-soundproof wall.

Life on the road is loud!

Back home to the hoped-for hush of our house. Not hardly! This apparent hilltop haven sits at the head of a canyon, which channels distant dins right into our den. The endless rumbling resonance of traffic on IH-35. The strident "Woo-Woo-Woohing!" of train, after train, after train. The peppy yells of summer cheerleader camps at the university. Even nearer is the natural neighborhood noise. Mowers mowing. Blowers blowing. Commuters coming and going.

Life at home is loud!

Maybe the ranch will relieve the racket. Wrong! Remote as it is, the world still whirrs by. A mile away runs a semi-major highway. On summer nights the sounds of a steady string of "semis" streaming through the open windows interrupts slumber. An air lane overhead swarms with the whine of high-soaring jets during the day. And frequently after dark, low, low flying military transports and helicopters on maneuvers squelch the serenity with the "whomp-whomp-whomp" of whirling rotors and the throaty growls of burly motors on the prowl.

And even during the lulls between these outside intrusions, native noises make their presence known. A caterwauling chorus of coyotes. The shrill, scale-climbing cacophony of cicadas. The blustering bellowing of bulls. The blatant blast of a braying jackass.

Life at the ranch is loud!

At times like this I conclude, "Ron, if you had to have a hearing loss, *now is the time*! Be thankful your hearing aid has an 'Off' switch!" So I turn the knob and hear the satisfying "click," which muffles and muzzles the distracting disquieting dissonance.

Does this fulfill my quest for quiet? Not quite!

As the outer uproar subsides, an intrusive inner invasion begins. Immediately I am reminded that there is no "Off" control on the mind!

A storm of thoughts thunder in. A squall line of concerns rains upon my brain. The wailing waves of a mental monsoon flood my stream of consciousness. Rafts of raucous responsibilities unresolved wash in, depositing discordant debris of duties undone. The teeming throng of disorderly intruders clamors for attention. My mind reels from the barrage of babbling bedlam. They scream, "Column deadline tomorrow!" They screech, "Speech day after tomorrow!" They squawk, "Shear goats next week!" They squeal, "Family vacation next weekend!"

Even a life of silence is loud!

With inner and outer ears ringing from the entire jangling clangor, I cry out, "God, life is too loud! This 'surround-sound' world is about to get to me. Can't you turn it off? Or at least tone the volume down a little? How do you expect me to hear your still, small voice amid all this deafening noise?"

At once a booming voice comes out of—somewhere. "WELL, RON SOMETIMES I DO WHISPER! BUT OTHER TIMES I HAVE TO HOLLER TO GET ATTENTION! IF YOU CAN'T HEAR ME IN THE SILENCE, LISTEN FOR ME IN THE NOISE! AS I'VE SAID OVER AND OVER AGAIN, 'HE, WHO HAS EARS TO HEAR, LET HIM HEAR!"

Momentarily stunned speechless, I finally manage to mumble, "I'm not sure I wanted to hear that."

UNBEEEEEVABLE!!

Jim Wacker is dead. UNBELEEEEVABLE!!

That trademark exclamation of Jim's describes the feelings of we who knew him. It's hard to believe that at the relatively young age of 66 this lively liver of life has breathed his last due to an insidious cancer that even his indomitable spirit could not defeat.

After his death on August 26, 2003, the media was filled with tributes to and memories of this legendary football coach who was probably the best known Lutheran in Texas. These are some of my thoughts.

It was my privilege to be the P.A. Announcer for Southwest Texas State University football when Jim led them to two consecutive NCAA Division II National Championships in 1981 and 1982. During that time, my wife and I became close personal friends with him and his wife, Lil. That relationship waned somewhat when they went off to coaching positions at TCU and Minnesota. But it blossomed anew when Jim returned to San Marcos in 1998 as Athletic Director at SWT, and they bought a house three doors down from us.

Conversations with him were always peppered with "UNBELEEEEVABLE!!" which he used in the sense of "astounding," "incredible," "amazing." And that is exactly the word I would use to describe him. Jim Wacker was one UNBELEEEEVABLE guy!!

The story is told of a football coach who was relieved of his duties and at the ensuing press conference made the statement, "I leave this position the same way I began it—fired with enthusiasm!"

That fit Jim Wacker to a tee. Good times and bad, he was the most enthusiastic person I have ever met. Winston Churchill once described Franklin Roosevelt by saying, "Meeting him is like opening a bottle of champagne!" The same could be said of Jim. His sparkling, bubbly personality made him a delight to all who drank of his presence. As someone said, "Talk about a sunny disposition—you could get a tan just listening to Jim."

The word "enthusiasm" has its roots in the Greek "en-theos," which means "to have God inside." That, too, describes Jim Wacker. He was a deeply spiritual man of faith.

When word got out that Wacker had been hired as Athletic Director at SWT, Don Hood, the track coach at the time, commented, "This is like a church praying for a preacher and getting God!" (To which then football coach Bob DeBeese responded, "I'm glad to know I'm working for God—he forgives!")

Coach Hood may have been closer to the truth than he realized. One of my favorite quotes by Martin Luther is, "Each Christian is to be a little Christ."

Jim Wacker was a "little Christ." (Although "little" is not a term often associated with Jim— except for his ego.) Someone has said, "The best way to send an idea is to wrap it up in a person." God was wrapped up in Jim's life, and he had the remarkable ability to unwrap that gift, to let the "God inside" out.

One of the things I have heard over and over and over again about Jim was the incredible inspirational influence he had on others. "Inspiration" is defined in my dictionary as "a divine influence upon human beings."

Brad Buchholz wrote about Jim, "He lived with an enthusiasm that spilled out of the glass and cascaded outrageously across the table." The "God inside" could not be bottled up in Jim's life. The cork was constantly being popped, the effervescence showering down on all around.

Emile Zola wrote, "I am here to live out loud." And, boy did Jim Wacker do that! Every time he opened his mouth, out came a pep talk. He was a master of inspirational speaking, in private as well as in public.

At Jim's funeral, Roosevelt Collins, who played for him at TCU, told about a recruiting visit. "Coach Wacker came into my living room and talked for 45 minutes—straight. Later my mom asked if he was a coach or a preacher. My dad said whatever he is, it was a heck of a sermon."

But Jim was not all words. He practiced what he preached. Rollie Martinson, who presided at the funeral, read a letter from Wacker's ten-year-old grandson, Karl, who wrote, "You taught me so much. You were still happy even though you knew you were going to die. I hope I can do half of the good things you did in your life. I'll be a better person because of the lessons you gave to me."

Amen, Karl. You speak for all of us who were fortunate enough to experience the divine influence that poured out from the God inside your Granddad.

Jim Wacker. Enthusiastic. Inspirational. UNBELEEEEVABLE!!

What if You had a Funeral and Nobody Came?

It was a nice casket. A very nice casket. Solid oak, it was designed for viewing by large crowds.

The registry book, however, contained the signature of only one visitor.

With forty-five minutes remaining before the scheduled burial time, the minister sitting in the funeral home parlor all alone with the casket kept having the reoccurring thought, "What if you had a funeral and nobody came?"

He knew the deceased had requested a modest funeral with only family and close friends. He knew the family was honoring that request with only a graveside service. But he had still expected some people at the funeral home prior to the service—at least the family.

It came time to transport the body to the cemetery. Still no family. No visitors.

The casket was loaded into a Suburban and began its ten-mile journey to the burial site. The minister followed in his car.

When the two-car funeral procession arrived at the cemetery, there was no one there either. As the two funeral directors went to unload the casket, the older of the pair asked if the minister would mind helping them. Solid oak is heavy. He agreed, and the three makeshift pallbearers placed the casket over the grave.

Everything was ready. The only ingredient missing was an audience.

Finally, ten minutes before the scheduled burial, a car arrived. It contained four members of the immediate family. Shortly, four other vehicles drove up. The lone passenger of each was a family friend.

Polite greetings and condolences were exchanged. Then the service began.

Being true to the family's wishes, the minister kept it short and simple. An opening prayer, obituary, scripture, a few intimate words of consolation, another prayer, the committal of the body to the ground, the benediction—it was over and done in fifteen minutes.

A few more minutes of visiting and remembering, then the cars and their occupants went their separate ways.

The incident reminded me of a story Liz Carpenter tells in her book *Getting Better All the Time* (Simon & Schuster, New York, 1987).

Seems as if a lady in New York plotted her daily walk by a funeral home so she could use the handy powder room. Each day she signed the book at the door as a matter of courtesy. Once, to her surprise, she received a call from a lawyer informing her she had inherited $25,000 from an old gentleman whose will bequeathed his money to whoever came to his funeral. She was it.

"What if you had a funeral and nobody came?" Such a thought would have been unthinkable in the rural, small town environment in which I was raised.

Funerals were community affairs. Within hours after someone died, neighbors bearing food began to appear at the family home. Friends came to sit with the body round the clock. Businesses would close during the funeral and the entire community would turn out to say "Goodbye" to their neighbor.

Death is never an easy thing to go through for the surviving family. But the caring support of friends and neighbors can ease the pain and lighten the load. There is comfort in community.

Families who go through a death alone have my sympathy. They may hear the assuring good news that there is life after death. They may read the Gospel words that God loves them and is with them as they walk through the valley of the shadow. And I'm sure these words bring some solace.

But words alone, no matter how beautifully written or eloquently spoken, can never take the place of the "word made flesh"—the warm, caring hugging, helping, smiling, crying, loving, living presence of sympathetic people.

The Ice Cowpades

I thought I had heard every sound there was to hear on our ranch. But this was a new noise.

Snuggled under the electric blanket, clad in turtleneck sweater, long-handles, socks, and stocking cap, I was not ready to leave those cozy confines and investigate what was going on in the cold world outside.

But then the strange sound that had awakened me repeated itself. CRUNCH! CRUNCH! CRUNCH!

Now let me make it clear, this was no "captain" crunch. Not even a "major" crunch. This was a "five-star general" crunch! And it was right outside my bedroom window.

Curiosity overcame the concern for the cold. Flipping back the covers, I slipped into my sheepskin slippers and went to the window. Peering out into the dawning light, I gazed on a world turned white overnight. The predicted ice storm had hit with a vengeance. Ground and grass and trees were covered with sleet and ice.

The CRUNCH! sounded again. Looking toward its source, I saw a half-dozen cows walking around the yard fence. With each hoof step, their one thousand pounds plus of beef cracked the two-inch sheet of ice with a thunderous CRUNCH!

Relieved to know I was not being attacked by the fierce residents of Jurassic Park, I lit the fires in the house and dressed in my warmest winter uniform. After a quick breakfast, I went outside to investigate first hand the transformation of our Red Hill Ranch into the White Hill Ranch.

I was greeted by one humongous skating rink. The ice covered everything. Sliding my way to the yard gate, I found I couldn't get out. The latch was frozen. A couple of resounding whacks released it, and I gingerly walked to the pickup. It was one giant ice cube. The doors were welded shut by a quarter-inch wall of ice.

I tried to figure out how to break through all that without damaging the truck. Then, looking at the ground under the tires, I realized it really didn't matter. Even if I got into the cab and the engine started, that vehicle wasn't going anywhere on such slick traction.

So I decided to walk to the barn and feed the cows.

Gingerly covering the slippery two hundred yards, I got a sack of range cubes and poured them out on the ice. It was then that the show began.

As the hungry cows went sliding and crunching after the elusive edibles, it reminded me of an amateur version of "The Ice Cowpades." The choreography did leave something to be desired, however. There were no Olympic medalists this day on this ranch rink.

And there was even a little hockey involved. With a lot of heavy "body-checking" going on, the ravenous bovine tongues flicked out toward the tempting tidbits. To their frequent surprise, however, the cows' usually dependable appendages did not always bring the mealy morsels back to their mouths.

Instead, the tongues became mini "hockey sticks" propelling the cubic "pucks" across the ice. Fortunately the furtive feed usually ended up in the "net" of another cow's mouth. Eventually the entire herd was able to achieve their goal and eat their fill.

The sun came out before noon and soon the menacing ice was converted into meaningful moisture. The storm had been intense, but short lived.

It was around long enough, however, to remind me how glad I am to live and ranch where I do. I do not envy my agricultural brethren who live in climes where "The Ice Cowpades" is a daily performance during the winter months. An occasional one-night stand road show is enough for me, thank you very much.

It was also a reminder that I had very little to do with selecting the site of my ranch. That was a family decision. A great-great-grandfather choosing to leave his native Germany for Central Texas. A grandfather picking this particular piece of land. Me? All I decided was to stay close to my roots and keep the place.

Farmers and ranchers in cold country probably have much the same reasons for being where they are.

Which raises the reflective questions, "How did you get where you are? Where you live? Where you work? Where you church?"

WHAT MAKES YOU PURR?

The two retired reverends restfully rocked on the riverfront cabin porch. Faces glowing from the reflection of the setting sun off the tranquil water, they blissfully savored nature's twilight serenade.

A breath of breeze gently strummed the wood-shingled roof with fingers of live oak leaves. The bass of bullfrogs joined the tenor of tree toads in throaty harmony. The featured soloist, a mockingbird, chirped a merry melody from a nearby mulberry tree.

In the midst of this serene symphony, a sleek calico cat sauntered around the corner of the cabin. Ambling up to one of the rockers, it nimbly leapt into the lap of the occupant. The cat's back made a couple of caressing passes across the passive pastor's belly, its tail tantalizingly tickling his nose. Then after a few moments of ministering to the minister's thighs with massaging paws, the flirtatious feline folded itself into a ball and settled down. Cozy and comfortable, the contented cat began to purr.

The gentle vibrations flowed from the animal into its human host, spreading soothing serenity from scalp to sole. The lulling lullaby rippled across the space between the rockers. Fluttering into my ears, the placid purrs passed their peace on to me.

It was then I understood why friend Tex Luther had named his longtime pet "Purrly Gates." The ol' puss' purring presence had opened up a peek into paradise for a pair of pooped preachers.

As we slowly rocked, basking in this heavenly moment, Tex broke the reverie. "Ron, what makes you purr?"

"You mean like ol' Purrly Gates is doing right now?"

"Yeah. What gives you such pleasure and satisfaction, such peace and contentment that if you could, you would just curl up like this ol' cat and turn on the purr motor?"

"Easy question," I quickly answered. "That's exactly the way I feel right now. Sitting quietly with a friend on his cabin porch after a lip-smackin', belt-bustin' mess of fresh fried catfish."

"But when else? What else?"

Taking a moment to shift from digestive process to thinking mode, I began to voice the first things that came to mind. "At a holiday table soaking up the pleasurable presence of all my immediate family...Absorbed in a good book...At the ranch during a hot, dry August, listening to the welcome tattoo of rain on a tin roof...Hearing hearty applause after a speech...On vacation with nothing to do, and all day to do it...Licking an envelope to the editor containing a completed column..."

As I paused in my list of purr-fect moments, Tex interrupted. "Speaking of columns, if you wrote about this experience—which you probably will—how would you tie it into a faith message?"

Switching gears once more, I again went with the initial image that appeared on my mental monitor. "I'd use Purrly Gates as a role model for me and my relation to God. Whenever I realize I don't have to run after the mouse of salvation, or run from the dog of sin; whenever the awareness fully sinks in that there is a gracious God who feeds me with love and defends me with forgiveness; that is when I take a lesson from ol' Purrly. I leap into God's protective lap, contently curl up, and celebrate the pleasure of his company with a peaceful purr."

"Now it's your turn, Tex. What makes you purr?"

The rocker went forward and back before Tex responded by pointing to his lap and saying, "I purr when Purrly purrs." Rock. Rock. "If I were a writer, I'd use that as a model of human relations. Purrs produce purrs." Rock. Rock.

"And then?" I asked.

"And then I'd shut up and let the reader do the rest."

Taking the hint, I quietly rejoined Tex in his rhythmic rocking. And shortly thereafter we both joined Purrly, all three peacefully purring our cares away.

THE CAT IN THE CASKET
(In Grateful Memory of Pastor Wilfred Menke)

We don't always know how church traditions begin. But sometimes we do know exactly when and why they end. For example, the practice of the casket remaining open during funeral services at St. Martin's Lutheran Church, a small town Texas congregation.

When Forrest Kreinautlaudt came to be their pastor, he was surprised that somehow this tradition had become the norm at St. Martin's funerals rather than the usual Lutheran custom of closing the casket prior to the service. Even though personally uncomfortable with the practice, he was wise enough to know it was not an issue worth making waves over.

So the new pastor went along with the local tradition. He did, however, begin asking families whether they wanted the casket open or closed, explaining they did have that option.

In Pastor Kreinautlaudt's first five funerals there, no one chose to change the custom. But during the sixth funeral, a sudden, abrupt change of opinion occurred.

It was a warm August morning when the congregation came to pay their last respects to Otto Oldenschott, a longtime, revered member. The family, as expected, had opted for the traditional open casket during the service.

The little church had no air conditioning. But raising the windows and opening the front and back doors created a pleasant draft, making it quite comfortable inside.

The pastor had just begun Psalm 23 when he felt something brush against the bottom of his robe. Looking down, he was shocked to see a cat rubbing itself against his robed legs. It was a neighbor's old yellow tom. The cat frequently hung around the church and had apparently walked inside through the open back door.

Without missing a beat in his reading, the minister began, with gentle backward sweeps of his foot, to try to move the intruder off to the side. He pushed the cat away while in "green pastures." But the tom was back before the "walk through the valley." More subtle kicks again moved the cat aside in "the presence of my enemies." But before the pastor could relax, the old tom returned to "dwell in the house of the Lord forever."

So far the congregation was not aware of the little drama going on behind the pulpit. They just thought the perspiration appearing on the minister's face was due to his heavy robe.

The struggle between flustered pastor and feline friend continued on through more scripture reading until finally, with an emphatic kick during "he who believes in me shall never die," the cat did not return.

While the next hymn was being sung, Pastor Kreinautlaudt anxiously looked around. Seeing no sign of the cat, he sighed with relief, returned to the pulpit and began his sermon.

All eyes were intent upon the preacher. But soon, one by one, heads began to turn toward the casket. As they did, eyes got wider, and more than one mouth dropped open in wonder.

Curious, the pastor followed the gaze of the congregation. To his amazement he saw sticking up out of the casket, a yellow tail, rhythmically going back and forth! The old tom had not gone outside. He had just found another more receptive object of his affection.

Preacher and worshippers, all were transfixed by the sight. No one moved a muscle or made a sound.

Finally, the organist, Hulda Musicker, who was closest to the scene, took action. A crusty country woman noted for always knowing the right thing to do in a crisis, Hulda got off her stool. She walked over and grabbed the cat by the scruff of his neck. Lifting him out with one hand, she gently closed the casket with the other. Then Hulda marched to the nearest open window and calmly deposited the cat outside in his rightful domain.

Remarkably all those present retained their composure during the entire incident. The pastor quickly ended his sermon. And with a short prayer the funeral was over.

But as soon as the mourners were outside, they began to quiz one another. "Did you see what I saw?" When all their answers agreed, they rushed to their cars and pickups, off to spread the news to those unfortunate enough not to be present.

From that day forth the incident of "the cat in the casket" became a part of local legend and lore. And at St. Martin's Lutheran Church no one ever again asked for an open casket during a funeral.

A Helluva Way to Get to Heaven

I don't like suffering. Anything the dictionary defines as "something painful or unpleasant," with synonyms like agony, misery, distress and torment – that is not my idea of a good time.

Nor is suffering my idea of a blessed experience, something given to us for our own good, to help us grow spiritually and draw us nearer to God. Frankly such a thought sounds to me like a helluva way to get to Heaven!

But then, what do I know? Who am I to argue with Paul's words in Roman 5: 3 and 4 (NRSV); "We...boast in our sufferings, knowing that suffering produces endurance, and endurance produces character, and character produces hope..." So I guess I need to re-examine my idea of suffering.

It was a common attitude in Bible times that suffering came as punishment from God. And a lot of people still believe that today. But Paul denies that. He says suffering is a sign of God's love. That suffering has within it the opportunity for spiritual transformation.

"The Book of Job," observes comedian Bill Maher, "is all about Job asking God to take away pain and misery. And God says, 'No. I can't. I can't take away pain and misery because then no one would talk to me!'"

Misery loves company, especially the company of a comforting God. Suffering reminds us of our human limitations, that we can't handle everything in life by ourselves, that we need help, divine help.

Paul assures us that when we need God, God is with us. And with that presence comes endurance, character and hope.

Endurance is the ability to hold up under the pressure of pain and unpleasantness. The stamina, the nerve, the guts to stomach a disagreeable and / or frightening experience.

Character comes from a Greek word describing the process where metal is purified by fire. The intense heat purges out all the base materials, giving the metal a strength it did not have before.

Hope is the energizing encouragement that comes from surviving a fiery furnace. This builds a rugged confidence and sturdy trust that with God's presence, *victims of* suffering can become *victors over* suffering.

A cancer patient was once rudely asked how it felt to be dying from cancer. Her quick reply, spoken with a smile was, "I am not dying of cancer. I am living with cancer!"

To me, that is a marvelous, positive attitude. Confronting the crisis of suffering from the viewpoint of not what it is going to do to you—but rather, what you are going to do with it. I admire and applaud people who approach the problems of life with such an optimistic outlook. I hope I am one of those people if and when suffering stops at my doorstep.

I hope I will be able to practice what I preach, to listen to Paul and look for the comfort of God's company in my misery and receive the peace that presence brings.

I hope I will be able to see the positive possibilities in an apparent negative experience. If somewhere along the line I do hear a dire diagnosis, I hope I will recall the old Rule of Thumb: "Bad news is never as bad as it sounds at first." I hope I will remain optimistic, heeding Norman Cousin's advice: "Nobody knows enough to be a pessimist."

And through it all I hope I won't forget those other words of Paul, "All things work for the good of those who love God." I hope I will trust God to know what's best for me. And then have the realistic faith to follow Larry Winget's counsel: "Expect the best. Plan for the worst. Celebrate whatever happens."

At the beginning I said I don't like suffering. After pondering Paul's comments, I really can't say I like it any better. I still think suffering is a helluva way to get to Heaven!

But I do find great comfort in the assurance that if my journey to Heaven does include a detour through the Hell of suffering, God will be my traveling companion. And that gives me hope that I will be able to endure the physical suffering and receive the spiritual benefits possible in such an experience.

In the meantime, however, I am going to add to my prayers that old Jewish petition: "May I never suffer all that I can endure!"

Practicing What I Preach

It was a good sermon—if I do say so myself!

The delivery was professional, displaying natural talents polished with years of training and experience. The content was solid. Just the right mix of sound biblical exegesis and sincere personal faith.

The response was positive and affirming. As the congregation exited, the routine comments of "Good sermon, Pastor," were laced with enough additional remarks to let the preacher know people had listened.

The message had been heard. The written words on pulpit notes had been transmitted through the preacher's voice to the ears of those in the pews, processed through minds into hearts, and now were being transported from the church building to homes and workplaces, taken out of the Sunday worship service to be translated into weekday service lived with family and neighbors.

Ron Birk, Communicator, had done his job. I was pleased. My seminary homiletics and New Testament professors would have been proud.

The sermon text was from the familiar "Walk to Emmaus" story: "They saw him, but somehow did not recognize him."

After discussing some of the scholarly attempts to explain this lack of recognition of Jesus by his two followers, I admitted that I really don't know the answer to that mystery, but find it a fascinating question to speculate upon. It prompts me to wonder if Jesus is walking with me today—and I don't recognize him!

As I trudge along the road of life, forlorn and full of questions, is Jesus right here along side me? Do I see him, talk with him, walk with him, but still don't put his name with the face beside me?

And if not, why not? Is it because I am looking for Christ in some other form? Am I conditioned to expect the divine presence only in some supernatural, spectral, other-worldly apparition? Is my quest for God limited to burning bushes, vocal visions, talking clouds?

Do I forget that "the word became *flesh* and dwelt among us?" Do I need to be reminded of the clear biblical implication that Christ continues to be with us "in the flesh?" Do I need to re-read his words, "As you have done it unto the least of these my brethren, you have done it unto me?"

Have I lost sight of the fact that Christ is in my neighbor? That he speaks to me through human lips, listens to me through human ears, comforts me in human arms, and helps me with human hands?

Is it possible that Jesus is also walking with me on human feet—and I don't recognize him?

Preaching such a sermon is exhilarating, yet exhausting. Adrenalin kept me going until I got home. But there the effects of four hours round-trip travel, plus another four hours of supply pastor duties at two services and other intervening activities, caught up with me. Nap attack!

As I was headed for the refreshing sanctuary of my recliner, the phone rang. It was our son. "Dad, I've got some church questions I need your help with."

I was tempted to say, "Not now. I'm too pooped to be a Pop. Let me call you back after my nap." But I didn't. And for the next thirty minutes, fighting fatigue, dutiful dad listened as musician son shared the frustrations of his attempts to gain a wider audience for his jazz liturgy.

When the conversation ended, I started again toward my nap nook, only to be intercepted by my wife. "What was that all about?"

Wearily I summarized son's questions. "Did you help him out?" she asked. "I'm afraid not," I said. "They concerned matters I'm not up-to-date on. Plus, I was so tired; I don't think I was even a very sympathetic listener."

Then as I collapsed in the recliner, my wise wife, with a wry smile, commented, "But he talked. And you listened. Seems to me I heard something in a sermon this morning about God speaking to us through human lips and listening to us with human ears."

As my heavy eyelids dropped, the last thought before blessed sleep was, "Preaching is easy. But *practicing* what I preach, that ..."

STUFF!

I like humor that makes me laugh for a minute and then makes me think for hours. A specialist in this kind of comedy is "the thinking person's comic," George Carlin. One of his classic routines is on the subject of "Stuff."

"Stuff is important," say Carlin. "You gotta take care of your stuff. You gotta have a place for your stuff...That's what life is all about, tryin' to find a place for your stuff! That's all your house is: a place to keep your stuff...while you go out and get...more stuff! 'Cause that's what this country is all about. Tryin' to get more stuff. Stuff you don't want, stuff you don't need...Even stuff you can't afford! Gotta keep on getting' more stuff. Otherwise someone else might wind up with more stuff. Can't let that happen. Gotta have the most stuff!" (From *Brain Droppings*, Hyperion, New York, 1997).

I don't have the most stuff—yet! But I still have a mess of stuff. Especially at our ranch, where, during three generations of Birk ownership, houses and storage areas have become stuffed with stuff.

There is stuff that at one time or another has been necessary for the day-to-day operation of the place: tools, supplies, home furnishings, etc. Added to this stuff is stuff from each generation's house in town. Stuff that wasn't good enough to keep there anymore, but "too good to toss out. So let's just take it to the ranch."

Combine that with the inherent rancher's atti-tude, "never throw any stuff away. You might need it someday," and it is sure as shootin' that after so long a time, storage space will become saturated with "more stuff than you can shake a stick at."

This obvious truth was brought home recently when I went to unload a pickup full of incoming stuff. There was "no room in the inn." Neither of the two houses or the two storage sheds had any remaining space. So I ended up at the barn. There, after a dusty reshuffling of old stuff, I was able to stuff in the new stuff.

Standing back to admire my creative cramming, a creepy thought crept into my cranium, "That's nice, Ron. But where are you going to put the *next* load of stuff?"

While cogitating on that unsettling thought, the preacher side of my brain kicked in. "Hey, Ron. This remind you of anything in the Bible? The Parable of the Rich Fool, maybe? The one where a farmer has such good crops he runs out of storage room. So he considers replacing his old stuffed barns with bigger new ones. Then he'd have plenty of space for his current stuff, and maybe even some more stuff as well. With a stock of stuff like that, he could live a long, good secure life.

"But then God gives the ol' sodbuster a rude wake-up call. 'You fool! This very night you will have to give up your life. Then who's gonna get all this stuff you've piled up for yourself?'"

Finding oneself smack dab in the middle of a real life modern version of an old Biblical parable can get your attention! It can cause you to wonder with Phillip Gulley, "Is our willingness to cast things away a measure of our spiritual well-being? Consider this: the first thing the followers of Jesus did was leave their stuff behind. Jesus said to Peter and Andrew, 'Follow me,' and immediately they left their nets and followed him." (To which, Gulley adds this side comment, "Peter and Andrew were not from around here. Otherwise, they'd have had a garage sale first.")

"He also asked the rich young ruler to leave his stuff behind, which the young man couldn't bring himself to do. He loved his stuff too much and went away sad. From what I can tell, it's the only time anyone ever went away from Jesus sad." (From *For Everything a Season*, Multnomah Publishers, Sisters, OR 1999).

That's good stuff to remember for those of us who are tempted to think, "Happiness is a barn stuffed with stuff."

As a result of all this heavy reflection, I am proud to report that I have decided *not* to build any new barns at the ranch. Now all I have to do is figure out what to do before the next load of stuff arrives.

We Have NOT Always Done it This Way

"Jesus Christ is the same yesterday, today and tomorrow." I believe that by faith.

The same, however, does not hold true for the "body of Christ." The church of today is not the same as it was yesterday. I know that by experience.

In my fifty years in that part of Christ's body called "Lutheran," I have seen lots of changes, especially in worship. The following are some personal remembrances of the way things were in the 1950s. This list is not to imply that what we Lutherans did then is "better" than what we do now—or vice versa. It is merely an observation, meant to remind "old-timers" and "newcomers" alike that we have *not* always done it this way.

- In the vast majority of congregations, except for Lent, Christmas, and maybe Advent, there was only one weekly worship service—Sunday morning at 11.
- Before the service began, worshippers sat in silence. If they needed to communicate with each other, it was in a whisper.
- People "dressed up" to attend worship. Women wore hats. Men and boys wore suits and ties—even in unair-conditioned churches.
- Many, if not most, worshippers were in the same pews where their parents, grandpar-

ents, and maybe even great-grandparents were sitting or had once sat.

- Everybody knew everybody else.
- Ninety-seven percent of the members were "born" Lutheran. The other three percent had married a "born" Lutheran.
- Bulletins were mimeographed. Inserts were rare.
- Ushers ushered—and were "Men only."
- Acolytes were young males. They wore dress pants and shoes beneath their robes.
- Women's role in worship was—to worship. Unless they were the organist or sang in the choir.
- There was one "Order of Service"—the one "in the book."
- Guitars were for Bible Camp, not regular Sunday worship.
- The pastor(s) led the liturgy, made the announcements, and distributed the bread and wine during communion.
- The most common pastoral garb was a plain black "academic" robe. Although a few daring individuals wore cassock and surplice.
- A pastor wearing a clerical collar during Lutheran worship was probably a visiting Episcopal priest.
- Scripture lessons were read by the pastor, at the lectern, from the King James Version of the Bible.
- Preachers preached from the pulpit—using notes.

- The only "children's sermons" were those delivered in stern whispers by parents in the pews.
- The role of worshippers in public prayer was to say, "Amen."
- The only "passing of the peace" was a mother slipping a restless child a piece of gum.
- Communion (a.k.a. "The Lord's Supper") was once a month. In some congregations, quarterly.
- Altars were up against the wall.
- The "bread" of communion was a wafer. The "wine," usually Mogen David. Or in a few select congregations, homemade from wild Mustang grapes.
- The wafer went directly from pastor's hand to communicant's mouth. The wine was either served in the common cup or individual cups —no choice.
- There were no unconfirmed children at communion. In fact, no unconfirmed Lutherans, period.
- Following worship, "decaf" coffee was not an option during Fellowship Time—mainly because it had not been invented yet. In fact, most churches had not yet invented Fellowship Time.
- Also after worship you could usually find a group of old-timers lamenting all the changes in the church and saying, "We didn't use to do it that way."

Never Ask a Rancher the Size of His Spread

The horse munched grass as I sat on his back with one leg hooked over the saddle horn, leisurely using my "Texas dental floss" (a toothpick) to remove the remnants of the hearty cowboy breakfast.

As it got lighter I could see other riders sitting at about quarter-mile intervals across the rolling plains. We were waiting for the rest of the roundup crew to finish the sweep of the pasture and bring the cattle by us on the way back to the distant corrals.

My Central Texas eyes were still adjusting to this West Texas view. In my native area of tree-covered hills and canyons, gathering livestock is a ride and seek affair. Here it is all ride. No seek necessary, as the cattle have no place to hide in this treeless expanse.

On a weekend speaking engagement in Odessa, I was staying with one of the old-time ranching families of the area. Thinking a Hill Country rancher might like to see how things are done on a West Texas ranch, they had asked me to join them as they moved a bunch of heifers from one pasture to another. Eagerly accepting their gracious invitation, I was thoroughly enjoying myself.

Along with the difference of the lay of the land, the other thing I immediately noticed was the *amount* of land. Where I come from we talk in acres. Out here they speak in sections. (A section being 640 acres.)

As I sat in the saddle gazing out over the vast vistas of my host's spread, I couldn't help but wonder about the size of their outfit. But in spite of my curiosity, I knew better than to ask them how big it was.

One of the first articles of the "Code of the West" I learned as a country kid was, "Never ask a rancher the size of his spread." If he wants to offer that information on his own, fine. But you never ask. That is considered to be impolite and nosey.

So ingrained is this rule, that whenever outsiders unaware of the code ask me, "How big is your ranch?" the temptation is to curtly respond, "That's none of your business."

But I don't. Mainly because of another article in the western code, "Always be polite." Instead I smile and make some evasive remark like, "Well, it's too big for me to take care of it. But not big enough for it to take care of me."

The questioner usually gets the message, smiles back, and moves on to another subject.

Which raises the point—all of us have things in our lives that are personal and private. Matters that are "just between me, God, and the fence post." Any probing into these delicate areas by unknowing outsiders is considered rude and insensitive.

For example, the state of one's soul. A lot of people, me included, get a little touchy when some over-zealous inquisitor, full of religious verve and nerve, starts poking around the tender spots of one's spiritual life with all the delicacy of a well-digger performing a root canal.

How do you respond to such callous invasion of privacy, and do it in a polite, Christian manner?

One way might be like a former campus ministry colleague of mine working among the evangelistic fervor of a Deep South community. When confronted with the brazen question, "Brother are you saved?" his response was to say, with a smile, "Well, I'll be damned if I'm not." And then walk away.

The lesson? Before you start asking questions of others, first question yourself about your questions. Remember the good advice, "If you want to stay out of trouble, be careful what you say." (Proverbs 21:23 GNB)

On the other hand, if you are on the receiving end of such ignorant interrogation, don't forget your manners. Be gracious and polite in your response, recalling the wise counsel of another proverb, "Give a silly answer to a silly question, and the one who asked it will realize that he's not as smart as he thinks." (Proverbs 26:5 GNB)

THE CHURCH IS A MESS

Sitting at his antique roll-top desk, Tex Luther was a mirror image of the miniature replica of Rodin's "The Thinker" perched on one of his shelves.

I could tell he was in that zone of creativity we preachers get into sometimes. Knowing how rare those moments are, I felt reluctant to disturb him. But lifting chin from hand, elbow from knee, he turned to me with a welcoming grin and said, "Come in. Come in. Before we go golfing (I had stopped by to pick him up), sit down. I've got something I want to share with you."

Easing myself into the comfort of an old cane-bottom rocker, I asked, "What's up?"

"The church is a mess," Tex gleefully replied.

Seeing my raised eyebrows and quizzical look he quickly added, "That's the title of the sermon I'm working on for next Sunday." (Even though retired from full-time preaching, Tex filled in occasionally at a nearby congregation.)

"Run out of old sermons?"

"After forty years? Not hardly. But out of the blue came this great idea I'd never thought of before. Want to hear about it?"

"'The Church Is a Mess'? You bet. I definitely want to hear where you're going with that."

Picking up his notes from the desk, Tex said, "I'm starting with the dictionary and its definitions of the word 'mess.' One of those is: 'a state of trouble or difficulty.' Seems to me that's a predicament most humans find themselves in all too often. Next, turning to my trusty thesaurus, I found all kind of common phrases we use to describe that situation: 'In a pickle.' 'Behind the 8-ball.' 'In hot water.' 'Up the creek without a paddle!'"

Jumping in, I added "'The fat is in the fire.' 'Between a rock and a hard place.' 'Got your tail in a crack.'"

"Right, Ron. You get the idea. Now to me those are all graphic, everyday expressions that describe the Biblical teachings about sin. We're all in a 'mess.'"

"What about that other definition of 'mess'?" I asked. "You know, the 'unclean,' 'dirty,' 'soiled,' connotation of the word?"

"Ties right in," Tex said. "The church is a bunch of 'messy' people. Sinners."

"OK. I'll go along with you so far. Where are you going from here?"

"'To another entirely different meaning of the word 'mess'—'a meal or dish.' Expanding on that definition, my dictionary says 'mess' is: '(a) a group of people who regularly have their meals together; (b) the meal eaten by such a group; (c) the place where it is eaten.'"

"The church is a 'mess hall'!" I almost shouted, feeling like a contestant on a game show. "Now there's something to think about."

"And there's more," Tex went on. "How about the phrase 'mess around', which means 'to get involved.' What does that have to say about the mission of the church?"

"Another thought provoker," I agreed. "Anything else?"

"Yes," Tex smiled. "The real kicker for me was the discovery that the words 'mess' and 'message' are related. They both come from the same Latin root word, 'missio,' which means 'to send,' as in 'mission.'"

"Sounds to me like your mission has been to find a message in a mess."

"Well, I am excited about all the 'messes,' dishes, I've come up with. Now I just hope I'm chef enough to put them together into an exciting, savory meal. Any suggestions?"

"Not really. Except how about this for a closing summary: The church's mission is to mess around in messy situations with messy people giving them a mess of the message of the Messiah."

"I don't know," laughed Tex. "Then I might have to say to you what Stan Laurel used to say to Oliver Hardy, 'Another nice mess you've gotten me into.'"

Pausing as he realized what he'd just said, Tex grabbed a pen and quickly wrote it down on his note pad. "Hey, that just might work as a tie-in to evangelism."

Standing back, he looked at the jumble of paper and books before him, turned to me and said, "Time for a break. Let's go mess around on the golf course. After that maybe I'll be refreshed enough to come back and make a message out of this mess."

BIRTHDAY PRESENTS

My birthday at the ranch began with the arrival of the season's first cool front bringing with it a brisk breeze, overcast skies, light drizzle and 50-degree temperatures.

Arising early, I lit the ancient propane space heater to combat the chill in the far-from-airtight frame house my parents built in 1941. Soon the room became toasty cozy. Warm moisture appeared on the cool window panes. I brewed a cup of hot tea, burrowed into an heirloom mission-style chair, which my body has savored for over sixty years, and wiled away the time until it became light enough for me to begin the day's outdoor chores.

When silhouettes of oak trees finally began to appear outside, I went into the kitchen and had a healthy breakfast of fiber-filled cereal and "lots of pulp" orange juice. Then into the bedroom, there to don old jeans, long-sleeve shirt and waterproof boots.

Returning to the living room, a movement outside caught my eye. Rubbing the moisture from a window, I saw two acorn-fat raccoons ambling across the pasture and a curious young doe deer trailing along behind. Amused at this unusual parade, I watched until they disappeared in the high grass and mist.

Turning down the heater, I slipped on a jacket, grabbed my well-worn Stetson, and went out the back door. Just as I got to the yard gate, another doe whizzed by with a nice 8-point buck in close pursuit—a vivid reminder that the cool weather was warming up the annual animal mating instinct, that hunting season was near at hand, and that I needed to get things ready for the invasion of hunters only a couple of weeks away.

Cranking up the old pasture pickup, I drove the couple of hundred yards to the rock house my grandfather built for his bride back in 1905. Walking inside its 18-inch thick quarried-stone walls, I realized this was a better work site than the damp, raw outdoors. So I began the task of cleaning it up so hunter guests would have a reasonably respectable residence during their visit.

After a few hours of wielding a broom, sponge, and toilet brush, it was time for a break. Back to the frame house. Wash off the grime. Put on cleaner clothes. Climb into my road truck and make the 23-mile drive into Mason.

As I drove up the hill just south of town to the 1910-era house that my parents bought and renovated in 1954, the contractor was waiting. Fifty years of time had taken their toll. Repairs, replacements and additions were needed if the place was going to be a livable "second-home" for the current generation of Birks. That remodeling project was now in progress.

We toured the property as the contractor brought me up to date on what had already been done and what, as a result of the inevitable "surprises" discovered while working on an old house like this, still needed to be done.

I made a few obvious decisions myself. Others needed approval of the rest of the "building committee" (my wife and daughter). Saying I would get back to him on these items, I wrote the contractor a check for "work to date," and got back in the truck, made a late lunch stop for barbecued ribs, and returned to the ranch, where I resumed my cleaning chores.

That evening, back in my favorite chair, reflecting on what had transpired since last I sat there, the question came to mind, "Was this any way to celebrate my birthday?"

"YES!" was the instant answer. "I spent the day 'playing' with my birthday presents. Because that is exactly what the ranch and the place in town are —gifts of birth. I have them only because I was born —born to the previous owners, gracious parents who preserved and passed on these possessions to their only child—me. I am truly a gifted child. So what could be a more fitting birthday celebration than to use, care for, and enjoy these gifts of birth?"

Just as I really began to chew on the profundity of this insight, my thoughts were interrupted by a sly little voice whispering in my brain, "Well, with that kind of thinking, maybe next year you should spend your *baptismal* birthday in church!"

FAMILY WITNESS

It was Mother's Day. The teacher of the Parent's Sunday School Class thought he would liven things up by bringing in a special prop—a 40-foot-long I-beam, which he laid on the floor.

As the class began, the teacher asked a young mother, "If I gave you $20, would you walk across that I-beam?"

Without hesitation the mother replied, "Sure."

"Suppose the beam was suspended between two buildings fifty stories in the air," said the teacher. "Would you walk across it for $20?"

"No way," came the quick answer.

"OK," the teacher went on, "suppose I am on top of one of those buildings dangling one of your kids over the edge. You are on top of the other building. And I say to you, 'If you don't walk across that I-beam to get your kid, I'm going to drop him.' Would you do it?"

This time there was a long pause. Then the mother asked, "Which kid have you got?"

Those of us who are parents can probably identify with that mother's question. Most of the time we will do anything for our kids. However, there are those *other* times!

One of the first things you learn as a parent is – children can be little angels one moment, little devils the next. And as you both get older you discover the only thing that changes is "little" becomes "bigger." Children always seem to have the knack of taking their parents on a roller coaster ride of emotions, from the heavenly heights of happiness to the hellhole of heartache.

There is a story that after God created Adam and Eve, the first thing he said to them was, "Don't."

"Don't what?" Adam asked.

"Don't eat the apples," said God.

Sure enough, shortly thereafter, what did God see? His kids walking around chomping on some apples. "Didn't I tell you not to eat those apples?"

"Yes, you did," said Adam. Eve chimed in, "Yeah, you sure did."

"Then why are you eating the apples?"

The two replied in harmony, "Because we're hungry."

So God punished his children by commanding them to have children of their own!

Moral: If a loving and all powerful God has trouble with his kids, don't be too hard on yourself when you have trouble with your kids.

Robert Fulghum gives good advice when he says, "Don't worry that your children never listen to you; worry that they are always *watching* you!"

Lets face it, most of us learned to be parents not from reading Dr. Spock or going to a class on "How to be a Mommy or Daddy in Twelve Easy Steps." No, we learned about parenting by watching our parents raise us.

The Jewish Talmud says, "When you teach your son, you teach your son's son."

The example we set as parents affects not only our children, but also their children, their children's children, and who knows how many generations yet to come.

And our parental influence is even felt beyond the family. Someone has pointed out, "Our children are not going to be just 'our children.' They are going to be other people's husbands and wives—other people's neighbors—other people's employees or employers."

When Jesus said, "You will be my witnesses...to the ends of the earth," he just may have been talking to his followers about their roles as parents.

We are witnesses for Jesus when we relate to our children as God relates to his children—celebrating and rejoicing when they are angels, enduring and understanding when they are devils.

Simply put: witnessing, evangelism, spreading Jesus' good news of love, grace, mercy and forgiveness *begins at home!*

Take Your Boots Off!

Shep Moses watched the last woolyback jump out of the gooseneck trailer. Daddy-in-law Jethro Priest ought to be happy now. The sheep had been moved from his over-grazed pasture to neighbor Sy Nye's place. Here there was more grass. That should take care of them for awhile.

Just as Shep climbed into the cab of his dually pickup, out of the blue a storm came up. Thunder cracked. Lightning flashed. The wind blew. But to Shep's disappointment, it didn't rain a drop.

Quickly the storm was past. The sun came back out. Shep cranked up the engine and was getting ready to pull out when out of the corner of his eye he saw something burning.

Turning off the switch, he jumped out of the truck, grabbed a tow sack from the bed of the pickup, and high-tailed it toward the fire.

As he got closer, Shep could see it was a little-bitty ol' mesquite that had evidently gotten hit by lightning. Just as he was about ready to start swatting it with the sack to snuff it out, he stopped. Something was peculiar here. Then he realized what it was. The mesquite was on fire, but it wasn't burning up!

Taking his hat off and scratching his head, Shep slowly circled the tree trying to figure out what was going on. Suddenly he jumped back as a voice came out of the flames. "Moses!"

Goosebumps popped up on Shep's arms and neck. His eyes bugged out. His mouth dropped open. And again the voice said, "Moses!"

Shep's mouth was as dry as cotton, but he stammered out, "That's—that's me."

Then the talking tree said, "Take your boots off."

"Do what?"

"Take your boots off!"

Shep looked down. He was standing on a bunch of jagged rocks. There was prickly pear all around. Where there wasn't cactus there were grass burrs. Not far away was a big fire ant bed.

His old beat-up boots were the only thing protecting him from all this. Take them off, and Shep knew he was defenseless. Sock-footed there was no way he could run away from whatever that was in the fire.

But before he could cogitate much more on what to do, the voice blasted out again, "TAKE YOUR BOOTS OFF!" That did it. Shep knew authority when he heard it.

So carefully scraping off a little clear space in the dirt, he slowly lifted his leg and tugged off one boot. Gently putting down his stocking foot, he repeated the procedure with the other leg and boot.

Setting the pair up so nothing could crawl in them, Shep straightened up. Shifting from one foot to the other while the hot sand cooled off, with nervous toes twitching in his soiled, smelly, holey socks, and with occasional sneaky looks for invading ants, scorpions, or snakes, Shep stood there, bootless, and listened.

And as he did, he heard a lot of things he had never heard before. Revealing things about God and himself. Scary, challenging things about his future.

A lot of what Shep heard he really didn't want to hear. He argued. He protested. He made excuses. But bootless in the cactus, he had no choice but to stay and listen.

Finally when the voice was through, Shep was a changed man. And the change in his life changed the lives of a lot of other people. In fact, you might say it changed the whole history of the world.

The moral of the story? Sometimes the only way God can get us to listen to Him is to make us take our boots off.

A Hunting We Will Go

The door to the hunting blind slowly opened. A blaze-orange-cap-covered head appeared, followed by a body clad in camouflage coveralls. Once outside, an insulated gloved hand reached back inside and pulled out a rifle. Double checking to make sure all the shells were out, the weapon was leaned against the blind. Back inside the hand went, emerging with a backpack and an empty coffee thermos.

Creakily straightening up, old pastor friend Tex Luther gathered his stuff and put it in the back of the pickup. Opening the passenger side door, he and his empty rifle joined me in the warm and cozy cab.

Putting the truck in gear, I moved on to pick up our other pastoral buddies scattered through the pasture.

"Well, how was it?" I asked.

"Great!" replied Tex with a smile. "Gorgeous sunrise. Brisk, but comfortable weather. Listened to a couple of owls hooting 'goodnight' to each other. Watched a family of raccoons retire into a hollow log. Then the day shift began to arrive. A covey of quail stretching their wings. A jackrabbit licking its paws. A pair of squirrels playing hide-and-seek with each other round and round the trunk of a big oak. It was a marvelous morning. Until..."

"Until what?"

"Until a bunch of deer came along!"

"But that's why you're out here, right? To hunt deer," I said.

There was a pause before he answered with a sheepish grin, "Not really. Not anymore. In my macho younger days, filling my tags was goal number one. Now, however, that's not on my list of reasons for being here at all."

"So, why are you here?"

Again, a pause. Then the thoughtful answer, "Two reasons mainly. One, to be with the guys. To enjoy the camaraderie and fun of bonds forged over twenty years of having this annual week together. And, second, to be alone. These two hours in the early morning and again in the late afternoon all by myself in a blind, what a welcome break from a normal, noisy, people-filled routine. In a very real sense, this is a spiritual retreat for me, and I find myself looking forward to these times of silence and solitude all year long."

"So you don't plan to take a deer?" I asked.

"Oh, yeah," he quickly replied. "My family expects some venison. And I need proof that I really was deer hunting. But I'll do that later in the week. Now I'm just going to un-lax. Watch nature's show and during the intermissions maybe read and even write a little."

"Do any of that this morning?"

"Well, as a matter of fact I did. Jotted down a few thoughts on how pastors know they are hunters. For example," and here he pulled out a wrinkled piece of paper and began to read:

"Pastor, You Might be a Hunter If...

...you think the liturgical color for November and December is blaze orange.

...your rifle is cleaner than your desk.

...a pastor friend receives a call, and you wonder whether it's for deer or turkeys.

...you have a Bible with a camo cover.

...you have ever paid for a hunting lease with continuing ed funds.

...you can play 'A Mighty Fortress' on a hunting call.

...you think 'healing the blind' refers to repairing a deer stand."

About that time we pulled up to the next deer blind, where another pastoral buddy was already outside waiting for us.

As he joined us in the cab, I inquired, "Get anything?"

"Naw," he said. "Saw several deer. But nothing I wanted. Maybe tomorrow."

With that Tex and I began to laugh.

"What's so funny?" our newest passenger asked.

To which Tex replied, "We were just talking about you!"

WHEN THE SIZZLE FIZZLES

Wife Alberta and I recently had lunch at a café in Austin. It was a trip down nostalgia lane.

When we were college students at Texas Lutheran in Seguin back in the early 50's, our idea of the ultimate date was to pool our money, pile into my 1939 Ford with another couple and ply the 50 miles to the southern outskirts of Austin.

Our destination? Hill's Café—*the* steak house in Central Texas (at least to our novice gourmet tastes). Our quest? "The Sizzler"—a brawny sirloin, blusteringly served on a hot platter, bubbling in its own juices. A steak you could not only see and taste and smell, but also hear.

Oh, sure, it cost a whopping $2—but for that kind of total sensual experience, it was worth the sacrifice.

Years passed. Other eating establishments blossomed in booming Austin. Hill's dropped off our list of places to dine. Then radio personality Bob Cole took over the café and word was it had been restored to its former glory. We decided to check it out.

Full of memories, we walked through the door. The ambiance was down-home friendly. The menu was full of beef. And, yes, "The Sizzler" was still the featured entrée—a bit more than $2, but reasonable by today's prices. I ordered it.

Over salad, Alberta and I reminisced about past visits. The more we talked, the more my anticipation grew. By the time I saw the waiter approaching with our meal, my taste buds were worked up, my ears were perked up, ready for a blast from the past.

As he set the platter down in front of me, an obvious look of disappointment evidently appeared upon my face. Catching it, the waiter asked, "Is anything wrong, sir?"

"Uh, yeah. I ordered 'The Sizzler.'"

Caught off guard, the waiter paused before patiently replying, "This *is* 'The Sizzler.'"

Looking to Alberta for help, I saw a knowing grin and a reassuring nod. Then the embarrassing realization hit me—the steak was sizzling. I just couldn't hear it!

Apologizing, I sent the waiter on his way. After a moment to recover, I picked up knife and fork and began to eat.

At first I missed the stirring sound I had expected. But soon the tangy taste of the steak made me forget it. I ended up having an enjoyable eating experience. The sizzle may have fizzled, but the savory flavor saved the day.

All of which is a commentary on my life. At my current age stage, change has rearranged many previous priorities. One of these is the need for the "sizzles" of life—those rip-roaring, wild and wooly, hair-raising, spine-tingling, breath-taking events that thrill, arouse and stir up the body, mind, and soul.

The plain fact is: I am not as excited about excitement as I once was. This has affected my choice of recreation, entertainment and social activities. And, maybe most significantly, my involvement in the church.

Where once I was stirred up by high-powered, emotionally-charged religious events with pulsating music, rah-rah speakers and churning, cheering crowds, now such occasions are more apt to turn me off than on.

Such a statement is not meant in any way to put down those who find such affairs stimulating and inspiring. It is merely meant as an honest confession of one person's feelings. I don't defend my position. I simply state it as fact.

There is an old sales training cliché that says, "Don't sell the steak. Sell the sizzle." To those in the church who are consciously or unconsciously following this maxim, I would remind them—for those of us who can't hear the sizzle, you better sell the steak.

Our senses may have become dulled, our tastes may have changed—but we're still hungry. We still need meat. We still appreciate flavor.

Hill's Café has "The Sizzler" on their menu. They have, however, enough marketing savvy to also offer the same steak with the option to "hold the sizzle." I hope those who plan the church's menu have the same wisdom.

A PREACHER'S SUNDAY MORNING

6:00 AM	Alarm clock rings
7:00 AM	Pushed out of bed by spouse
7:15 AM	Fix cup of coffee
7:20 AM	Go over sermon notes
7:25 AM	Rewrite sermon notes smeared by spilled coffee
8:00 AM	Leave for church
8:15 AM	Drive back to parsonage and pick up sermon notes
8:20 AM	Leave tire marks on driveway speeding back to church
8:25 AM	Knock down "Reserved for Pastor" sign as car skids into parking lot
8:31 AM	Worship begins
8:42 AM	Last worshipper arrives
8:45 AM	Leave pulpit to go to office and pick up sermon notes
9:01 AM	End sermon abruptly when realize last page of sermon notes still in office
9:13 AM	Prepare communion bread and wine
9:15 AM	Strain muscle breaking communion loaf
9:17 AM	Can't find bearded man's mouth with chalice
9:29 AM	Bump into baptismal font during recessional
9:40 AM	9:30 Sunday School class begins
9:52 AM	Last Sunday School student arrives
10:01 AM	Ask class to read Bible verse together

10:02 AM	Discover each member has different translation of Bible
10:10 AM	Asked, "Where in the Bible is The Apostles Creed?"
10:16 AM	Class member comments, "If Jesus knew what was going on in this church, he'd turn over in his grave!"
10:29 AM	Bell rings to dismiss Sunday School
10:29 AM	Asked, "Before we close, could you quickly tell us the difference between 'pre-millennialism' and 'post-millennialism'?"
10:38 AM	Begin robing for 10:45 service
10:39 AM	Phone rings, crying woman walks into office, and acolyte asks, "Will you tie this rope around my robe?"
10:45 AM	Bell rings to signal beginning of worship
10:46 AM	Race to back of church, robing on the run
10:47 AM	Acolyte can't find matches to light candle-lighter
10:48 AM	Borrow matches from smoker outside on church steps and light candle-lighter
10:49 AM	Walk halfway up aisle and relight acolyte's candle-lighter
10:54 AM	Walk to altar and tell acolyte to forget about lighting candle, which has its wick covered with wax
10:55 AM	Begin liturgy

10:56 AM	Observe time of silence
10:56 AM	Cell phone rings. Caller asks, "What time does worship begin?"
11:03 AM	Last worshipper arrives
11:10 AM	Reach high point in sermon
11:10 AM	Child on front row gets up to go to rest room
11:14 AM	Repeat high point of sermon
11:14 AM	Child returns from rest room to front row
11:21 AM	Begin Communion portion of service
11:22 AM	First worshipper leaves
11:31 AM	Spill wine on richest member's white shirt
11:33 AM	While helping clean him up, spill rest of wine on his wife's fur coat
11:46 AM	Sing wrong verse of recessional hymn —loudly!
11:48 AM	Greet exiting worshippers
11:49 AM	Smiling worshipper comments, "That's the best sermon I ever heard."
11:50 AM	Frowning worshipper comments, "That's the worst sermon I ever heard."
12:12 PM	Last person leaves church
12:15 PM	Lock church
12:16 PM	Start thinking about next Sunday morning

THOUGHTS AT 65

"We will need a certified copy of your birth certificate to complete your application to begin receiving Social Security benefits." That request opened not only a bank lock box, but also memories and meditations from the document therein.

For example, the entry signed by the physician: "I hereby certify that I attended the birth of this child who was ALIVE..."

I learned how significant that word ALIVE was over forty years later, after my mother's death. An aunt shared a story that my parents had never told me. How they had wanted a child from the beginning of their marriage, but for some reason had been unable to make that happen. Finally, nine years later, the seed was planted.

The gestation period, however, was not easy. My mother had an extremely tough pregnancy. Once during a bout with uremic poisoning, the doctor had gone so far as to suggest an abortion to save her health, maybe even her life. But she would not hear of it, and with the aid of my aunt, a nurse, made it full term.

The drama was still not over. During delivery it was discovered that the umbilical cord was wrapped around my neck—three times! There was great danger I would choke. Somehow that complication was overcome. Little Ronnie took his first gasping, crying breath and was born—ALIVE!

Needless to say, after hearing that story I have had an even deeper sense of gratitude toward my mother. I am alive because someone really, really wanted me. Wanted me so badly that she was willing to go through great suffering and pain just so she could experience the joy of my presence.

Was I worth all her effort? Did I fulfill her expectations? Did I bring her the joy she deserved? From my point of view, I have my doubts. From hers, who knows? Mothers often see positive aspects of their children, which the children never see themselves. But one thing we both saw, agreed upon and rejoiced in—I was a loved and a *live* child!

Another entry reads: "Date of Birth: October 24, 1935."

Sixty-five years since my perilous introduction to this thing called life. How's it been? Well, so far it's been a fairly healthy trip. No long-lasting physical ill effects after that shaky start.

It also has been a life filled with love. A father who, in his own totally different, masculine style, loved me as much as my mother did. A wife who, for reasons as mysterious as those of my parents, has lovingly stuck with me for over 45 years. Two children who, each in their own way, communicate that their bonds to me are much more than mere physical genes.

And through it all there has been that still, small, loving voice of God. Whispering from my inner self, or speaking through the mouths of other people, words that repeat over and over the message, "Ron, you are special. You have innate talents. Unique gifts. Use them."

These are words I need to hear, want to hear. But, quite frankly, words I often dread to hear. With the comfort of affirmation and encouragement also comes the discomfort of duty and responsibility.

"To whom much is given, much is expected." This injunction has haunted me since early childhood. And even more so after learning how close I came to not receiving the gift on which all my other gifts are dependent—the gift of life.

Have I lived up to the giver of this gift's expectations? Have I loved as I have been loved? Has the talent of communication been put to fruitful use through my sermons and speeches, columns and books? Have I been a good steward of the land, houses, animals, and other assets received through inheritance?

Here, too, I have my doubts. But I also have faith in a God who looks at me through the eyes of a parent. Therefore I trust that just as on October 24, 1935, I was a loved child of Bess and Willis Birk, so on October 24, 2000, I am a loved child of God. And until that time when my birth certificate is joined in its resting place with my death certificate, I will continue on with the comfort and hope, the duty and responsibility of one who is loved and alive.

ABOUT THE AUTHOR

Retired after twenty years as Lutheran Campus Pastor at Texas A&M and Southwest Texas State Universities, Ron Birk now divides his time between the Texas Hill Country ranch near Mason, which has been in his family for over a century, and his career as a writer and speaker.

Ron has written four other books:

- *What's a Nice God Like You Doing in a Place Like This?*
- *You Can't Walk on Water If You Stay in the Boat*
- *St. Murphy's Commandments*
- *You Might Be In a Country Church If...*

Birk is also a popular humorous after-dinner speaker appearing before various types of groups around the country. For speaking engagement information contact:

Ron Birk

Mr. Ronald Birk
1597 Old Mill Creek Rd
Mason, TX 76856